James Garbarino
S. Holly Stocking

with

Alice H. Collins
Benjamin H. Gottlieb
David L. Olds
Diane L. Pancoast
Deborah Sherman
Anne Marie Tietjen
Donald I. Warren

Protecting Children from Abuse and Neglect

Developing and Maintaining Effective Support Systems for Families

Jossey-Bass Publishers

San Francisco • Washington • London • 1981

PROTECTING CHILDREN FROM ABUSE AND NEGLECT
Developing and Maintaining Effective Support Systems for Families
by James Garbarino, S. Holly Stocking, and Associates

Copyright © 1980 by: Jossey-Bass Inc., Publishers
433 California Street
San Francisco, California 94104
&
Jossey-Bass Limited
28 Banner Street
London EC1Y 8QE

Library of Congress Cataloging in Publication Data
Main entry under title:

Protecting children from abuse and neglect.

Includes bibliographical references and index.
1. Child abuse—Services—Addresses, essays,
lectures. 2. Child abuse—Services—United States—
Addresses, essays, lectures. I. Garbarino, James.
II. Stocking, S. Holly.
HV713.P76   362.7'1   79-24239
ISBN 0-87589-442-9

Manufactured in the United States of America

JACKET DESIGN BY WILLI BAUM

FIRST EDITION
First printing: February 1980
Second printing: May 1981

Code 8002

The Jossey-Bass
Social and Behavioral
Science Series

Preface

This book is for human service practitioners and public policy makers who are concerned about abused or neglected children and their families. Its aim is to lay the foundation for an approach to the problem that will recognize and strengthen the prosocial personal networks of families.

The idea emerged from two sources in particular: (1) research suggesting that parents who abuse and neglect their children often are isolated from neighbors and other personal social networks, and (2) research and anecdotal evidence suggesting that personal social networks, acting as informal social supports, can be powerful influences for change among abusing and neglectful parents.

We offer the volume at a time when many child welfare and social services agencies are searching for new, cost-effective, and efficient ways to cope with child maltreatment. The need for new approaches is clear. Since 1974, when Congress required states to set up procedures for reporting suspected cases of child abuse and neglect, human services agencies have been swamped with reports of child maltreatment. Each of these reports must be investigated and, if conditions warrant, served through an appropriate combination of supportive and protective services. Unfortunately, few of these agencies have been given the funds to manage this increase in case loads, with the result that many agencies have been stretched beyond their limits to perform. In Oregon recently, a child abuse caseworker was suspended without pay for a month as punishment for failing to investigate a reported case of maltreatment within the mandated seven days. (The child's body was found soon after.) In many counties of the same state, personnel of human services agencies have become so beleaguered that they have had to rely on law enforcement officials to investigate reported incidents. And so it goes from state to state. In some areas, the state welfare office has been forced to turn to private agencies for help in handling the cases it has received, but those agencies in turn have not been able to meet the demand for services. Many referrals have been turned away. Cases are often closed prematurely. Other individuals must wait months before they are assigned to a caseworker.

But staggering case loads and insufficient funds are not the only problems plaguing these agencies. In many cases, even when sufficient funding has been available, the ability of human services organizations to cope with the problems has been disappointing. As the authors of a recent evaluation of federally funded treatment programs point out, most child abuse and neglect programs probably cannot expect to have much more than a 40 to 50 percent success rate with their clients (Berkeley Planning Associates, 1978). Even when in treatment, some parents continue to abuse and neglect their children. Others go back to mistreating their children when the formal treatment program has ended. For all the public outcry against maltreatment, many children remain unprotected and their families left to their own inadequate devices.

The approach presented in this volume builds on the view that child abuse and neglect are problems not only of individuals but also of environments. It seizes on a natural social resource—friends, neighbors, and relatives of families-in-need—to help prevent and treat child maltreatment. And in so doing, it offers battle-weary practitioners and decision makers a promising tool for coping with a very difficult problem. The contributors to the volume come from a variety of perspectives. Some are psychologists, some sociologists. Some are primarily scholars, others primarily practitioners. They differ in the vocabularies they use to describe personal social networks, some referring to "informal family supports," others to "natural helping networks" and "natural social networks." They sometimes suggest differing strategies for creating and supporting social networks. But together they provide the rationale for a "social network" approach to combating child maltreatment and highlight many of the issues that practitioners and policy makers must face in adopting this approach.

The editors would like to thank numerous human service practitioners in the Omaha area for reading and commenting on earlier versions of the manuscript. Their suggestions reflected the concerns of a cross-section of professionals—hospital and public health nurses, child protective service workers, family service association staff members, community mental health workers, and others—and they were enormously valuable. Thank you, Barbara Jessing, Martha Skrocky, Gay Angel, Morgan Hecht, Paul Magin, Kathy Nelson, Mary Ellen Brown, Karen Martin, Deanna Haack, Peggy Tighe, Kathy Glazer, Mary Cramer, Susan I. Hardisty, Mark Hanna, John Weeks, Janice A. Rashid, Sister Judean Schulte, and Virginia Aita.

We would also like to express our gratitude to Gwen Gilliam, associate producer/writer at the Boys Town Center for the Study of Youth Development, for copy editing a previous version of this manuscript, which was published by the Boys Town Center for Youth Development under the title of *Supporting Families and Protecting Children* (1978); to Bess Melvin, Mary Pat Roy, and Daria Sweazy for the patience, persistence, and speed of their word processing; to James H. Sweetland and Betty J. Schnase for their excellent library services; and to Sandra Wallentine, Sandra Hutson, and Elizabeth J. Penke, Barbara Carson, and Nancy Jacobson for shepherding this manuscript through many versions.

Special thanks go to Thomas Gregory, director of the Research Use and Public Service Division of the Boys Town Center, whose contagious enthusiasm got this book off the ground; and to Nan Garbarino and William D. Timberlake, whose patient support helped make it a reality.

Finally, we are indebted to the Boys Town Center for its funding of this effort. The views expressed here are not necessarily those of the center or of Father Flanagan's Boys' Home, the nondenominational corporation that supports the center, but they do represent one of many efforts these enterprises are making to help children, youth, and families.

It is our hope that this book will help readers think a little bit differently about the social origins of child abuse and neglect and about social solutions to these very pressing problems. We caution, though, that this is not a cookbook with "tried and true" recipes for action. We offer this book as stimulus—one that we hope will help in the long struggle to support families and protect children. We recognize that frontline workers and decision makers bear the heavy burden of devising and implementing specific strategies to support families, and it is to them that we dedicate this book in the hope that it will help them shoulder that burden.

Boys Town, Nebraska   James Garbarino
November 1979   S. Holly Stocking

Contents

xi

The Authors

James Garbarino is associate professor of human development at The Pennsylvania State University and a Kellogg Foundation National Fellow for 1981–1984. He was awarded the B.A. degree in government from St. Lawrence University (1968), the Master of Art's in Teaching degree from Cornell University (1970), and the Ph.D. degree in human development and family studies from Cornell University (1973). He is the author of two other books and more than forty articles dealing with child welfare, social development, and education and is a member of the Society for Research in Child Development and the American Psychological Association. In 1975, he was named a Spencer Fellow by the National Academy of Education. His principal research interest is the ecology of human development and child welfare.

S. Holly Stocking is a science writer who specializes in writing about social science research for nonscientists. She was coordinator of Science Writing Projects for the Boys Town Center for the Study of Youth Development until September 1979 and produced a variety of publications—including newspaper and magazine articles, pamphlets, and posters—for practitioners who work with children, youth, and families, and for the general public. She has been a reporter and free-lancer for several nationally known newspapers and news services, has written many technical articles on the public communication of science, and has delivered a number of talks about science communication to national science and journalism organizations. She was awarded the B.A. and M.A. in journalism from Northwestern University (1966 and 1969, respectively); she is currently completing her doctoral dissertation on the public communication of science at Indiana University.

Alice H. Collins is a social worker in Portland, Oregon, and a consultant to a number of research and demonstration projects across the United States. The author of several social work texts, she began her exploration of natural helping networks and the relationships between professionals and such networks in a research project on family daycare.

Benjamin H. Gottlieb is an associate professor at the University of Guelph, Ontario, Canada and is currently a visiting professor at the University of Maryland, College Park. As a community psychologist, he has had a long-standing interest in the health-protective effects of informal support networks in the natural environment. Currently, he is conducting research on the effects of social support groups among new parents and on the role of mutual help groups in the human services. He is also preparing a book on social networks as informal support systems.

David L. Olds, a developmental psychologist, is director and principal investigator of the Prenatal/Early Infancy Project in Elmira, New York. In addition to research on the effects of maternal and child health interventions, he has designed and evaluated innovative programs in the area of educational psychology.

Diane L. Pancoast is a social worker and research associate at the Regional Research Institute for Human Services, Portland State University. She is interested in the ways individuals make use of their personal support networks and in the implications of natural helping networks for social welfare policies and services.

Deborah Sherman is an associate researcher on the Children's Policy Research Project of the School of Social Service Administration, University of Chicago, and an instructor of sociology at Roosevelt University. She formerly worked as an associate researcher at the Boys Town Center for the Study of Youth Development.

Anne Marie Tietjen, a developmental psychologist, is assistant professor in the Division of Family Studies, School of Home Economics, at the University of British Columbia. Her research interests include the social networks of parents and children and the development of peer relations.

Donald I. Warren is chairperson of the department of sociology and anthropology at Oakland University in Rochester, Michigan, and an adjunct research scientist at the University of Michigan. He is coauthor (with Rachelle Warren) of *The Neighborhood Organizer's Handbook* (1977) and has written extensively on neighborhoods and community structure.

Protecting Children from Abuse and Neglect

*Developing and Maintaining
Effective Support Systems
for Families*

CHAPTER 1

The Social Context of Child Maltreatment

James Garbarino
S. Holly Stocking

"If the only tool you have is a hammer, then you tend to treat every problem as if it were a nail." This figure of speech is powerful because it highlights the influence of technique on the way we define problems. But the same statement can be reversed: "If you see your problem as a nail, then the only tool you can use is a hammer." This rendering is especially relevant to child abuse and neglect, for efforts to solve the problem often are hampered by our perceptions of what the problem is.

In our society, we typically see child abuse and neglect—as we do all problems—as the result of an individual deficiency. We concentrate on parents who are mentally ill or have unrealistic expectations about what children can and should not do.

1

We focus on the pathological upbringing that makes a person unsuited for the demanding task of parenthood, or we look to the mismatch between parents' needs and children's needs. As a result of this orientation, we typically seek cures that emphasize individual rehabilitation and therapy. Without dismissing the importance of this individualistic perspective, and with full recognition that each case of child abuse and neglect has its own special origins, we would like to suggest that abuse and neglect are not *only* problems of individual abusers and their victims but are also problems of the social contexts in which these individuals live. We believe that, if we as a society can incorporate this idea into our thinking about the prevention and treatment of child abuse, we may be able to develop some solutions that will save both lives and dollars. In this chapter, we will present the rationale and evidence for this view as well as introduce some of the themes and topics that will be discussed in following chapters.

Social Context of Parent-Child Relationships

One of the most exciting developments in psychology in recent years has been the growing recognition that we cannot understand or appreciate human behavior apart from the social context in which it occurs—the same phenomenon, that is, can have quite different meanings in different contexts. Although most people continue to underestimate the influence of the situation on their behavior (Ross, 1977), psychologists now realize that the situation or social context in which an individual acts may be of critical importance. Researchers who study altruism have found that individuals who witness emergencies with other bystanders are less likely to intervene than those who witness them alone (Darley and Latane, 1968). Other researchers have found that children who "delay gratification" for less than a minute under one situation can be induced to wait ten times longer in another situation (Mischel and Ebbesen, 1970). This is not to say that individual characteristics are not important influences on behavior, only to say that it is the *interaction* between individuals and their environment that influences what people actually do (Bem and Allen, 1974). Developmental psychologist Urie Bronfenbrenner, who has been active in a wide range of social policy issues affecting families and children, is one of the leaders of this growing awareness of the importance of social context for behavior. His "ecological" approach to human development (Bronfenbrenner, 1977, 1979) highlights the importance of social context in many realms of human development, but particularly in parent-child relationships. Specifically, it posits the following six principles:

1. *Development in Context.* According to this approach, children and youth are profoundly shaped by their environments—by their families, friends, and classmates, as well as by their neighborhoods, their communities, and the larger culture. Similarly, parents are shaped by the settings in which they live. For example, in their classic study of Japanese, American, and Japanese-American families, Caudill and Frost (1975) found that mothers from the Japanese-American group treated their infants in a manner that demonstrated adaptation to American culture and a departure from Japanese culture. The ability of a parent to successfully raise a child is thus not simply a matter of "personality" and "character." Rather, it is also a function of the particular community and culture in which parents and children live.

2. *Social Habitability.* The ecological approach stresses the importance of "quality of life" for families and the importance of socially rich environments in creating that life. Parents, according to this perspective, need an appropriate mix of formal and informal relationships that can provide nurturance, guidance, and assistance in the difficult task of childrearing. Social policies and the practice of human service professionals should be directed toward enhancing the "social habitability" of environments in order to serve the interests of children. Thus, our concern vis-à-vis issues such as "parent education" must be to make the social environment of parents richer. It must focus not on "who cares for children, but on who cares for those who care" (Bronfenbrenner, 1978, p. 777).

3. *Mutual Accommodations of Individual and Environment.* According to the ecological approach, individuals and

environments make ongoing adjustments to each other; thus, if we are to understand human behavior, we should focus on the interaction of situation and individual over time. This has important implications for researchers studying human development. It demands approaches that can capture interactive effects, as well as longitudinal studies that go beyond one point in time. Willerman, Broman, and Fiedler (1970) conducted an excellent study that illustrates this point. They found that children who were developmentally delayed at three months were likely to end up mentally retarded at four years of age in low-income but not in high-income environments. Thus, early developmental delay may predict later retardation in one context but not in another. For policy makers and practitioners, this principle suggests the need for strategies that will address both individuals and environments, both "categorical" and "generic" needs, and that will do so on an ongoing basis.

4. *Second-Order Effects.* The ecological perspective tells us that many of the most important aspects of human behavior and development take place as a result of interactions that are shaped, even controlled, by forces not directly touching the individuals as they interact. Bronfenbrenner (1977) calls these indirect effects "second-order effects" to indicate that something beyond the two individuals is setting the agenda for their interaction. Relations between parents and children clearly are shaped by forces outside the family. What happens to the parent in the world of work affects both parent and children, even though the children never set foot in the work environment. Kohn's (1977) studies of how the work experience of men affects their childrearing values illustrates this. Men whose work requires following orders come to value obedience in their children, while men whose work emphasizes initiative value that same quality in their children.

5. *Connections Between People and Settings.* The ecological approach focuses our attention on (1) "ecological transitions," that is, the moves individuals make from one social context to another, and (2) "cross-contextual dyads," that is, the relationships that exist and work across different contexts, as when a child is both a student of and a neighbor to an adult or

when a social worker is in both a preventive and a treatment role. According to this perspective, parent-child relations are strengthened when child and parent share experiences in multiple situations—at home, in the park, on the ballfield, and so forth. It goes further, however, to tell us that the ability of parents to successfully raise their children depends in part on the level of richness of the social networks of both. When children have relationships with nonparent adults that transcend contexts and persist across time, parent and child are both strengthened. Thus, when children have enduring relationships with adults such as teachers, friends, neighbors, and relatives that continue as the children move from one setting to another and that exist in more than one setting, their development is enhanced (Cochran and Brassard, 1979).

6. *A Life-Course Perspective.* The ecological approach asks us to remember that both the meaning and significance of personality characteristics and situations may differ across the life course. For example, Bronfenbrenner's review of the effects of early social deprivation (1968) concluded that, while the immediate effects of maternal deprivation were most severe when such deprivation occurred in the second year of life, the long-term consequences were most debilitating for those institutionalized in earliest infancy. Parents who are very effective with young children may find themselves troubled when their offspring reach adolescence. Families that are highly dependent on neighbors for assistance with young children may find neighbors less helpful in coping with adolescents. The ecological perspective insists that few answers are correct across the entire life course. There are different answers for the same question, depending on the level of maturation of families.

The principal theme that emerges from an ecological analysis of parent-child relations is that the ability of parents to successfully raise their children depends in large part on the *social* context in which families live. It depends on the extent to which parents and children have enduring connections with others outside their home. It depends on the extent to which (and the way in which) outside forces intrude into the home and set the agenda for parent-child interactions. It depends on the norms of childrearing in the family's immediate environment. And it depends on where a family is in its life course.

This is not to underplay the importance of the economic context of parent-child relations. We know that income plays a significant role in affecting a family's social resources and the demands on those resources. Affluence permits the luxury of purchasing help to augment or complement one's existing informal resources. People with money can afford to join clubs, to attend social and sporting events with their friends, and to buy the necessary equipment for leisure-time activities. They can afford to eat out, to entertain, and to buy consumer goods, all of which increase the social contact that eases the stresses of daily living. Affluence, then, provides families with a hedge against personal deficiencies. It cushions. But it does so primarily because it supports, deepens, and enlarges the *social* systems that relieve individuals from their own personal failings. Affluence doesn't of course always have this positive effect. In extremely mobile middle-class families, the stresses of day-to-day life may be as overwhelming as they are for economically impoverished families. Studies of depressed women document this (Weissman and Paykel, 1974). Some very wealthy individuals are socially impoverished, while socially rich environments can emerge even in the most wretched of settings. But economic and social well-being do go hand in hand often enough to suggest that there is an integral connection between them. Recent national commissions on family life have documented the proposition that inadequate income remains the single most powerful indicator of *social* impoverishment for families (Kenniston, 1977; National Academy of Sciences, 1976).

From the ecological perspective, a critical need of parents —whether wealthy or poor—is for the nurturance and feedback that come from day-to-day interpersonal relationships. As human beings, we need friends, neighbors, relatives, and others to protect us when the demands of daily living become too pressing. We need our personal social networks to support and encourage us. As journalist Jane Howard describes her own social network in her book *Families* (1978): "We are numerous and connected enough not to let anyone's worst prevail for long.

For any given poison, our pooled resources can come up with an antidote" (p. 60). Naturally, a poisoned social network may be worse than none at all. In general, however, social networks are more antidotes than poison, more help than hindrance.

Social Context of Child Maltreatment

Much has been made of the individual characteristics of parents who abuse and neglect children. Numerous investigators have attempted to create a "profile" of the abusive parent. These researchers have cited a variety of personality characteristics and personal experiences that place an individual parent in danger of becoming abusive in his or her relationship with children (Spinetta and Rigler, 1972). Emotional deprivation in a parent's own childhood, low levels of empathy, low self-esteem, social aloofness, and a variety of other personal characteristics all contribute to make a parent "high-risk" for child maltreatment. From this perspective, the main cause of abuse and neglect lies in the individual parent. Abusive parents are different from nonabusive parents. They are pathological and may even require extensive psychiatric treatment to be "cured." The problem with this individualistic viewpoint is that much of the research it has generated is inconsistent and contradictory (Gelles, 1973). Furthermore, it doesn't tell us which "vulnerable" or "high-risk" parents will actually mistreat their children. Attempts to apply these individualistic profiles to the general population usually have not proved successful. Indeed, the most detailed and fully developed of these profiles designated some 60 percent of the general population at risk for becoming involved in child abuse (Helfer, 1978).

What transforms individual risk into abuse? The ecological perspective argues that it is the social context in which families live. More specifically, it is social and economic deprivation in the environment of families. Investigators repeatedly have demonstrated that social isolation is a correlate of child maltreatment (Bakan, 1971; Bryant and others, 1963; Elmer, 1967; Helfer and Kempe, 1976; Lauer, Ten Broeck, and Grossman, 1974; Smith, Hanson, and Noble, 1974). Parents who maltreat children prefer to solve problems on their own. They have few relationships outside the home, and they are likely to discourage outside involvements on the part of their children. They tend to be transient, at least in urban areas, and thus to lack enduring roots in their immediate environments. And they tend to have a lifelong history of avoiding activities that would bring them into contact with other adults. This does not necessarily mean that social isolation *causes* child maltreatment. But, social isolation is an indicator of potential trouble and often reflects a lifelong pattern of estrangement (Polansky and others, 1979).

Moreover, when combined with low income, social isolation may exacerbate the problem by making parents too dependent on social networks for assistance (Smith, 1977; Stack, 1974). At the very least, it facilitates and reinforces child maltreatment, for when families are divorced from personal "support systems" they are divorced from those sets of relationships that provide nurturance and feedback to individuals, that "tell the individual what is expected of him and guide him in what to do" (Caplan, 1974), and that provide him access to a variety of resources, both social and material (Cochran and Brassard, in press). In the words of Caplan (1974): "People have a variety of specific needs that demand satisfaction through enduring interpersonal relationships, such as for love and affection, for intimacy that provides the freedom to express feelings easily and unself-consciously, for validation of personal identity and worth, for satisfaction of nurturance and dependency, for help with tasks, and for *support in handling emotion and controlling impulses*" (pp. 4-5, emphasis added). Without enduring interpersonal relationships outside the immediate family, abused and neglected children may be marooned, without "allies" to turn to for help or protection. Likewise, abusive and neglectful parents may be cut off from potential sources of assistance and feedback.

Implications for Practice and Policy

If child maltreatment is grounded, at least in part, in the social context in which families live, then solutions to the problem must go beyond individualistic therapies and rehabilitation techniques to embrace personal social networks, neighborhoods, and communities. When viewed from this perspective, the essential question for practitioners and policy makers alike is no longer simply, How can we cure the individual pathology of a particular parent? It is also, How can we eradicate the pathology of particular environments? How can we foster environments (or "ecologies") that will relieve the social isolation of families and support successful parent-child relationships? How can we ensure that families-in-need are set within appropriately supportive social contexts? What can our governments—local, state, and national—do to ensure that people are not isolated from natural networks and that such networks are nurtured rather than undermined by official actions? And how can practitioners support and mobilize these resources on behalf of successful parent-child relations?

The contributors to this volume offer differing perspectives on these questions. But all converge upon the basic theme that efforts to strengthen the personal social networks of families may help to protect them from the hardships of life, whether these be of the family's own making or the creation of outside forces. For example, in her chapter on support systems in Sweden, developmental psychologist Anne Tietjen argues that families need both formal and informal systems of support, and that the challenge is to arrange things so that families have access to both. This requires a knowledge of what factors influence families' use of support systems, as well as an understanding of the individual family, the neighborhood and community in which the family lives, and the political, social, and economic underpinnings of these environments.

In the following chapter, Canadian psychologist Benjamin Gottlieb focuses directly on the personal social networks of families. Access to families, he argues, will be achieved only after intensive study of these networks, including the range of community settings in which families participate, the individuals who are trusted in those settings, and the culture of these trusted people. As we come to understand these factors, he notes, we may find that families that were formerly "hard to reach" now are accessible. In other cases, we may find that families lack the support of any social attachments. The challenge then is to break down the often considerable barriers that block the development of relationships.

Sociologist Donald Warren analyzes the neighborhood, which he defines and describes in terms of how people relate socially. He argues that neighborhoods vary according to the degree to which people identify with their surroundings, interact with one another, and relate to the larger community. These factors influence the neighborhood's problem-solving capacities, and practitioners who wish to influence or draw upon these capacities to support individual families must understand them. From Warren's perspective, professional interventions become synonymous with community development.

The rest of the authors offer suggestions for putting some of these perspectives into practice. James Garbarino and Deborah Sherman show how practitioners and policy makers can screen neighborhoods to identify areas that are socially impoverished and thus at risk for child maltreatment. They see a neighborhood approach to prevention and treatment as very promising. Given the social context of child abuse and neglect, as well as the increased pressures on human service agencies to put their money where it will do the most good, this approach may in fact be essential.

In separate chapters, social workers Diane Pancoast and Alice Collins describe how practitioners can identify "central figures" in personal social networks and mobilize them to support families at risk for child maltreatment. Practitioners in this approach do not help families directly but rather help the central figures, who either are (or could be) naturally linked to the target family. Finally, developmental psychologist David Olds cautions that efforts to strengthen informal social networks, while promising, should be but one part of a comprehensive strategy to address child maltreatment. He, like Tietjen, believes that a wide range of formal and informal community resources are needed to respond to the factors that undermine parents' abilities to appropriately care for their children. He describes and endorses an approach that is sensitive to personal social networks but that also incorporates systematic efforts to evaluate the relative merits of intervention strategies.

Potential Barriers

Readers who are in a position to affect programs or public policy on child maltreatment will quickly recognize that the barriers to strengthening the personal social context of families are many. Agencies and organizations often jealously guard their organizational turf and may be reluctant to relinquish some of the control they have over clients in traditional one-to-one relationships. Practitioners may be unwilling to share their functions with nonprofessionals. They may see central figures in personal social networks as incapable of dispensing help to needy families. New approaches that work to strengthen personal social networks may appear to be luxuries that most agencies cannot afford. What is more, efforts to promote and strengthen personal social networks raise the issues of confidentiality, autonomy, and privacy. What right do social workers and public policy makers have to meddle in people's daily lives? What right do they have to make prescriptions for families? Details on these and other barriers will emerge throughout this volume. But since the barrier of privacy *must* be faced by anyone who plans to put the approaches described here into practice, we would like to deal with it now in the hope of making clear the alternatives to privacy and the ethical implications of these alternatives.

To most Americans, the value of privacy is unquestioned. Invasions of privacy are tantamount to "cultural treason." This orientation is reflected in our laws, in speeches made by politicians, in the policies of private and public agencies, and in the opinions of citizens as revealed in public opinion polls. Privacy in the family is, in particular, a strongly held value. In fact, in few other realms of social life is privacy so cherished. Americans simply don't like to be told what to do behind the closed doors of their homes. How husbands relate to wives and parents to children is nobody else's business. Whenever we speak to public groups on child abuse and neglect, we can count on at least one person to linger near the podium afterward and recount an incident in which that individual became aware of child maltreatment in a neighborhood family but, out of fear of butting into another's private life, took no action. Well-schooled in the value of privacy, the potential good samaritan feels genuinely torn between not wanting to invade the neighbor's privacy and not wanting to let the child suffer.

The dilemma is real. But any thoughtful person will quickly realize that privacy, while valuable, has its costs. Indeed, our history and culture reveal a pervasive ambivalence about individualism and collectivism, freedom and authority, privacy and social integration. Webb (1952) called this ambivalence "the parabola of individualism." Philip Slater (1970) linked it to "the pursuit of loneliness," and David Riesman (1952) found it in "the lonely crowd." Americans place a high value on owning a single-family home, on the freedom a car brings, and on being independent of all regulations. It is as if we wished every man really were an island. Yet we decry the loss of community, the loss of nurturance and feedback that sustain individuals in times of stress. People become isolated, and isolation, as we have seen, creates a potentially dangerous context for parent-child relations. The individual who is concerned about the welfare of families must weigh the benefits of privacy against its potential costs. Does the "sanctity" of the home outweigh the right of children to live in environments that will allow them to develop to the best of their capabilities? Does the "privacy" of the family outweigh risks to a child's life? Does the risk of falsely accusing someone of mistreating a child outweigh the risk of abuse or neglect?

We think not. And we are buttressed in our belief by hundreds of thousands of cases in which children have been maimed or brutalized because friends, relatives, or neighbors were afraid or unable to interfere. Witness the following grisly case described in a story sent out over a national wire service (X, Y, Z, and A substitute for the actual names):

> Kansas City, Mo. (UPI) Police investigators said they could hardly remember a case worse than X's. Two- and three-inch strips of flesh had been torn from his face, arms, legs, back, buttocks and stomach; a purple bruise covered his chest; blood

soaked his shirt and pants by the time his step-father brought him to the emergency room.

Mr. X, twenty, was charged with second-degree murder and is being held on $500,000 bond. He signed a statement saying he hit X with his hand and a belt because he had not learned his ABCs.

Mrs. X, twenty-two, was charged with manslaughter by culpable negligence for her son's death. Her bond was set at $250,000.

Those who knew X often heard his cries and those of his two-year-old half-sister, Y, coming from the family's apartment. But they never thought, until too late, that he would die.

A string of "what if's" and "only if's" marred X's case.

—If neighbors had known about the twenty-four-hour toll-free answering service in the state capital for reporting child abuse.

—If the children's grandmother, Z, had not been rebuffed by state welfare officials for three months while trying to gain custody of the two children.

—If Mr. A, the postman, who lived above the family, had been more persistent when he told Mr. X not to beat the children. "He told me it was his kid and 'I'll do what I want.' I didn't bother him after that."

—If the mother's sisters, who knew that she was being severely beaten by her husband, had not been afraid of stirring up trouble by checking on the children [Garbarino, 1977b].

To readers who may have fears about violating families' privacy by supporting and becoming involved with personal social networks, we would like to make it clear that:

- Our principal goal is to help families succeed in caring for their children.
- We recognize the freedom that our society grants parents to make most of the important decisions in childrearing.

- Due process of law is designed to protect people from harassment and arbitrary action by human service professionals.
- Programs involving informal support systems will be locally governed and will respect local values to the extent that they are consistent with the best interests of children.
- Any loss in privacy will be more than made up for by an increased sense of community, mutual helpfulness, and neighborly concern.
- Rather than making human service professionals more arbitrary and intrusive, greater involvement with natural helping networks will make them more sensitive to the subtleties of family and neighborhood life. Friends, as many of our authors make clear, can be better helpers than strangers.

It is in this spirit that the authors offer their statements and proposals. We believe that, with care and intelligence, practitioners and policy makers can function without violating the rights, dignity, or integrity of the people they seek to help.

CHAPTER 2

Integrating Formal and Informal Support Systems: The Swedish Experience

Anne Marie Tietjen

The major theme of this book is that personal social networks, acting as informal family support systems, have an important role to play in strengthening families and thereby preventing the kind of social isolation that fosters child maltreatment. Personal social networks have always been the most basic means by which human needs for material and emotional support have been met. In modern societies, however, it is becoming increasingly common for many of the support services traditionally provided by kin, neighbors, and friends to be provided by public agencies. These agencies, institutions, or services may be viewed as formal family support systems. As such, they have an

15

important role to play in promoting social integration for families—a role that has been obscured by prevailing approaches to the design and delivery of social services. One of the goals of this chapter is to explore that role and to suggest ways of enhancing it.

As previously noted in Chapter One, research into the causes of child maltreatment has made it clear that the problem can be understood only in relation to the social context in which it occurs. Similarly, the integration of families into formal and informal support systems must be seen in context. Hence, another purpose of this chapter is to present a model for understanding the role of social, cultural, and personal factors in influencing the way in which families become enmeshed in formal and informal support systems. But we perhaps can better understand how these supports can be used to deal with child maltreatment in our society by turning to a culture different from our own. A particularly instructive example for this purpose is Sweden, with its highly developed system of social welfare, its well-articulated family policy, and its low incidence of child maltreatment and other forms of violence. While solutions to problems are related to their contexts just as much as the problems themselves are, and while they can seldom be transferred without modification from one environment to another, there is value in cross-cultural comparison of solutions to common problems. A major portion of this chapter, then, will be devoted to a discussion of social services, social networks, and the problem of child maltreatment in Sweden. Finally, some practical suggestions for dealing with the problem of child maltreatment will be made.

Nature and Functions of Family Support Systems

A personal social network has been defined as a "specific set of linkages among a defined set of persons" (Mitchell, 1969, p. 2). An individual is the anchor point for his or her own set of "linkages." Each link is a relationship between two people. It involves the anchor person and another individual, who may be a relative, friend, or neighbor. Mitchell goes on to say that "the

characteristics of the linkages as a whole may be used to inter-
pret the social behavior of the persons involved" (p. 2). In a
similar vein, Bronfenbrenner (1977) classifies the social network
as a social structure that encompasses the family and affects its
functioning. Some of the ways in which social networks influence family functioning are by providing information as well as
material and emotional support (Young and Wilmott, 1957;
Stack, 1974; Tietjen, 1977), enforcing social norms (Bott,
1971; Young and Wilmott, 1957; Stack, 1974), and offering
opportunities for stress-releasing social recreation.

Holter (1976) identifies an essential difference between
personal social networks and other types of human systems:
"The social network is an informal and fluid phenomenon with
a minimum of organization, partly because of changing participants and changing types of interaction or transaction. The network is bound together by a common culture and common
norms and can, in certain situations, constitute the basis for
organized actions, but in such a case loses the characteristic of a
social network" (pp. 193-194, author's translation). Organized
action is the usual purview of social services. Social services are
technically defined as "collective interventions which are outside the marketplace to meet the needs of individuals as well as
to serve the corporate interests of the wider community" (Rein,
1970, p. 47). Two major categories of services are health and
welfare services and cultural-recreational services. The former
category includes clinics, welfare offices, childcare services, and
various kinds of rehabilitation services. The latter includes
libraries, community recreation centers, and gathering places.

In our society each service agency typically performs a
highly specialized function. There is seldom any real integration
among the various services, even when they are dealing with
common problems. The emphasis on treatment of specific problems rather than on their prevention is part and parcel of this
approach. This imitates the medical model in responding to
human needs—a model that emphasizes treating sickness rather
than promoting health. By adhering to this medical model in
dealing with social problems, however, we have overlooked an
important potential role that social services of all kinds can

play. In providing supports to families and thereby reducing the isolation that contributes to such problems as the maltreatment of children, social services could play a key role in preventing these problems. While we will continue to need services directly concerned with treating families for whom child maltreatment is a problem, we also need to become aware of the potential of other kinds of services for helping to prevent the problem. This awareness can lead us to find ways to bring about real improvement in the lives of troubled families.

Both social networks and social services can function as family support systems by providing their members or users with nurturance, feedback, models of behavior, and opportunities to diffuse stress. But each has some important functions of its own as well. On the one hand, social services often have access to greater social and material resources for dealing with specialized problems than do social networks. They are usually staffed by specially trained professionals who can deal efficiently with particular problems and give informed, constructive feedback to parents. In addition, they can serve as an impartial third party, protecting the interests of both parents and children. Personal social networks, on the other hand, offer the possibilities of continuity over time, breadth and depth of relationship, mutual choice, and, perhaps most importantly, the opportunity to contribute as well as to receive.

While there are particular advantages associated with both formal and informal support systems, there are also disadvantages and drawbacks to each. In our society, people often are reluctant to use public health and welfare services because they dislike the impersonal manner in which services often are delivered and because they fear that they will be blamed for their problems and seen as inferior or incompetent. Many of us see such services as being the last resort for those who have no private means for solving their problems. But involvement in informal social networks can also have disadvantages in certain circumstances. Some individuals may have excessive demands made on them by their network members, or families with limited material or emotional resources may become overly indebted to their network members, a condition that they may find uncomfortable. These and other situations can strain a mutually supportive relationship to the point of dissolution.

Clearly there are some support functions that can best be provided through interpersonal relationships, others that are best performed by social service agencies, and many that could be provided by either. The available evidence suggests that even in situations in which support could be provided by either source, people in our society prefer to seek support from members of their personal networks rather than from social services. Croog, Lipson, and Levine (1972), for example, found that patients recovering from heart attacks sought aid from relatives, friends, and neighbors but almost totally ignored service institutions, with the exception of their physicians, even for tasks that might be performed more efficiently by institutions than by individuals. An important clue to understanding this preference is to be found in what increasing numbers of psychologists are coming to view as a basic characteristic of human nature; that is, people in most circumstances strive to achieve competence and control over their own lives and environments (see, for example, White, 1959). When we need support and assistance, we look to sources that will increase our feelings of competence and of control over our own lives. We turn to friends, relatives, and neighbors with whom we have relationships based on esteem rather than on authority, on reciprocity rather than on unidirectional aid. Support from relationships of that kind is more likely to enhance our feelings of competence and control over our own lives than is support from many formal support systems as they currently exist.

The crucial task, however, is to find the *right mix of formal and informal support*. We need formal services. The maltreatment of children is a problem in which intervention by service agencies is unquestionably necessary. The challenge lies in finding ways to make treatment and preventive services more responsive to the basic human striving to achieve competence and control over one's life. Services that assist people in this striving will be better received and more effective than those that themselves exercise control over the lives of the people they are meant to serve and support. Our goal in dealing with the problem of child maltreatment through the use of neighbor-hood social resources is to make it possible for families to be supported and enhanced through both formal and informal systems. If we are to know where and how to intervene in the interest of achieving this goal, we need to consider the conditions that influence social networks and social services and the ways in which families obtain support from them.

Understanding Family Support Systems

How is a family's use of formal and informal support systems influenced by society, the community, and the family itself?

Cultural and Ideological Factors. Ideas about politics, economics, and social life define the organization of society, and they influence the patterns of people's lives in very real ways. There are at least three such ideas that have a strong bearing on the nature of formal and informal support systems. The first of these concerns the nature of the relationship between family and state. In American society, this relationship is seen as a distant one. The family is regarded as an independent institution to which the state provides support only in emergencies or when private means have proved ineffective. This attitude serves as the rationale for the "medical" approach to service delivery and leaves the way clear for social isolation to occur. If, by contrast, family and state view their relationship as an interdependent one, with each party having a share in the responsibility of childrearing, as well as a stake in the outcome, measures to prevent social isolation and its related problems are more likely to be taken.

Closely related to the definition of the relationship between family and state is the way people view the distribution of economic resources in society. Poverty is a very real source of stress on individuals and families—stress that, in turn, promotes child maltreatment. Toleration of poverty also reinforces the victim-blaming attitude of many well-intended social service agencies. Those who believe that poor people are to blame for their own poverty are not likely to treat them with respect when dealing with the fallout from their economic condition, including child maltreatment. The nature of family support systems is also affected by ideas regarding self-sufficiency and interdependence among individuals. A norm that sanctions mutual helping among kin and neighbors provides a basis for strong personal networks. In modern societies, where conditions such as geographic and social mobility and the segregation of the world of work from the world of family are making it increasingly difficult for strong personal networks to be maintained, this same norm could serve as the basis for strong *formal* support systems.

Community and Neighborhood Factors. Many characteristics of communities and neighborhoods are influenced in varying degrees by the ideas discussed above, and these characteristics, in turn, affect a family's use of support systems. One such set of characteristics involves the demographic features of a neighborhood—its population, its size, and the distribution of the population across ages, ethnic groups, and socioeconomic levels. For example, a neighborhood with a homogeneous population tends to have greater interaction among residents than a nonhomogeneous neighborhood (Popenoe, 1974; Susskind, 1974). But perhaps most directly relevant to patterns of integration into formal support systems are the characteristics of the services themselves. Three such characteristics are especially important: (1) the actual functions of the services (what do they actually do?); (2) the accessibility of the services to the residents (how far must residents travel to reach the services in order to use them?); and (3) the method of service delivery (how does the agency define the relationship between itself and its users?).

Services differ widely in the way they define their relationship to their users. Users may be viewed as "customers" to be served, as "patients" to be cured, as "victims" to be rescued, or as "deviants" to be brought under control (Rein, 1970). Alternatively, users may be considered as participants in the process of service design and delivery. In this approach, users are encouraged to become involved with one another around issues of mutual concern and to take an active role in decision making. In addition to building feelings of competence and control in the participants directly, this method of providing formal services can help to build informal networks.

Family Characteristics. Relevant family characteristics can be categorized into two groups—those that influence a family's need for support and those that influence its ability to seek and get support. In addition, there are individual differences that make each family's adaptation to its circumstances unique. A family's need for support is affected by such circumstances as whether or not both parents are present in the home, whether or not any other adults are part of the household, the number of children in the family, the age and spacing of children, the socioeconomic status of the family, and the parents' employment situation. In addition, special needs of family members, frequent or recent events requiring adaptation or change, and the timing of major life events all contribute to a family's need for support (Garbarino, 1977a). In general, the more one needs support, the less likely one is to have the personal resources to obtain it. But personality variables such as locus of control and specific social skills are not always impaired by adversity. Families in great need of support often are able to meet their needs through social arrangements of one kind or another (Stack, 1974; Young and Wilmott, 1957).

How should we go about increasing the supports available to families? The best solution would be found in a society with a strong and active commitment to the social and economic well-being of families, a tradition of interdependence among families, and a strong system of social services that emphasizes user participation and encourages informal networks. One society in which at least two of these requirements are met is Sweden.

Social Networks and Social Services in Sweden

During the past 100 years, Sweden has made the transition from one of the poorest agrarian nations in Europe to a modern urban industrial society with one of the world's highest standards of living and a highly developed system of social welfare. A number of fortunate circumstances have contributed to Sweden's development. Among them are abundant natural resources, more than 160 years without war, a historical tradition of pragmatism blended with humanitarianism, and a population that was homogeneous until the recent influx of "guest workers" and other immigrants. While Sweden's economy is basically capitalistic, cooperation between the public and private sectors is extensive. Both personal and corporate taxes are high, but nearly one third of the total tax revenues is spent on social welfare programs. Social welfare legislation expanded rapidly during the forty-year period of Social Democratic government, and the new, somewhat more conservative government has continued to expand such programs.

Sweden's accomplishments in providing for its people are impressive. Poverty is almost nonexistent. Infant mortality rates are the lowest in the world. And, in a country of eight million inhabitants with an extremely efficient system of reporting and record keeping, only about ten children per year—most of them under the age of three—are hospitalized for maltreatment, and only "occasional" deaths occur as a result of abuse (Petersson, 1976). The number of reported cases of physical abuse per 100,000 population is roughly one fifth that of the United States (Lagerberg, 1977; Gil, 1970) despite Sweden's meticulous reporting and record keeping. One important way in which Sweden demonstrates its commitment to the welfare of its citizens is through its family policy. Based on the assumption that society as a whole benefits when one generation takes responsibility for the next, this policy is directed toward "a more equal distribution among various groups in society of the costs of the care and upbringing of children" and toward an assumption by society of responsibility for "tasks which, in an earlier system of production, naturally rested with the family" (Folksams Sociala Råd, 1976, author's translation). Emphasis is placed on a realistic acceptance of social change and the provision of supports to families in their existing circumstances.

Concrete manifestations of Sweden's family policy take the form of monetary allowances, various forms of work leave for parents, and social and recreational services. Allowances include a universal child allowance paid to parents of all children under sixteen (or still in school), a housing allowance based on family size and income (which is available to low-income families), and a furnishings loan for families-in-need. Nine-month paid maternity and paternity leaves have recently been made available by law. Services designed specifically to provide support to families with children include a homemaker service for use by mothers who become ill and cannot care for their children and for working mothers whose children become ill and cannot go to daycare centers. Holiday arrangements for mothers and children are subsidized by the state. Public funds provide preschools, daycare centers, after-school care centers, and mother-child clinics that keep in close touch with mothers and their infants from birth until the children enter school at age seven.

In addition to services directed specifically toward families with children, there are a number of other services and agencies that contribute substantially to the well-being of families. One of these is the welfare bureau, which provides financial assistance to those in need, occupational rehabilitation training, and treatment of alcoholics, as well as most of the child-related services mentioned above. Social and recreational services include supervised play parks, libraries, athletic facilities, and community centers that offer activities primarily for teenagers and pensioners. There are also numerous private recreational organizations that receive public subsidies. Finally, there are local medical and dental clinics. There is a great deal of cooperation among the various service agencies, and they try to prevent duplication of services. Despite the wide range of services provided in Sweden, however, the demand usually exceeds the supply. This is particularly true of daycare, homemaker services, and dental clinics. Thus, despite a national conviction that social services should be provided equally for all citizens and not just for those with special needs, the ideal is not a reality. Nevertheless, services are extensive and wide ranging, especially in comparison with those in the United States.

There are three strong values in Sweden that bear on the existence of formal and informal family support systems. First, there is a strong tradition of local autonomy and local control in Sweden. The demands of modern bureaucracy are undermining this tradition in the case of social services, however, and the relatively high mobility rates in urban and suburban areas make it increasingly difficult for local authorities to manage. Second, "managing for oneself" within the extended family is highly valued. This can probably be traced to a period when agrarian households, including extended families and hired help, had to manage for themselves because of a harsh climate and great distances between farms. This norm actually reflects a reluctance to ask for aid rather than a reluctance to give it, and its strength is primarily among older, more traditional Swedes. Finally, family ties are very strong in Sweden, and many urban families regularly visit their extended families in the country on weekends and holidays (Liljeström, 1975). Thus, values in Sweden seem to encourage the integration of its residents into both formal and informal networks of support. A closer look at urban neighborhoods in Sweden will show how these values are transformed into reality.

Services in Swedish cities tend to be distributed geographically in clusters, with each cluster serving several neighborhoods. Thus, while no urban Swede is completely without access to services, some neighborhoods are better equipped with services than others. Moreover, most local services do not take upon themselves the job of encouraging informal interaction among users. Nor do they provide means for user participation in most instances. At the level of neighborhood services, then, Sweden has not encouraged families to build strong networks among themselves or made universal active participation in formal support systems possible.

Within the last decade, Swedes have become acutely aware of the great potential for social isolation that exists for the many families who are new to the cities. Many of these families are housed in new suburban communities consisting of high-rise apartment buildings, often located some distance from the city center and even from shopping and other services. A number of studies (for example, Axelsson and others, 1971) documented the isolation and anomie among housewives in some of these communities, and these findings have led to attempts to solve the problem at the local level. The idea of encouraging interaction among neighborhood residents and user participation in social services has begun to take hold. Parents' organizations at daycare centers are becoming increasingly common. People who use community recreation centers now have a strong voice in the programs at these centers. Neighborhood children's clinics are currently experimenting with parent education groups, and a preschool program that actively involves mothers is emerging. But before I describe some of these new programs in detail, I would like to report briefly on a study I conducted in Sweden in 1976, when most of the new programs were not in effect.

Support Systems in Swedish Suburban Neighborhoods

In this study, I compared both the personal social networks of married and single mothers and their use of social services. The mothers were all residents of four suburban neighborhoods in Gothenburg, Sweden's second largest city. Sixteen families in each neighborhood were interviewed. Each of the families had at least one child in the second or third grade at the local elementary school.

The neighborhoods in the study were selected on the basis of a citywide inventory of service locations and published information about population characteristics. Two of the neighborhoods selected were classified as having high access to services (a wide range of services was within walking distance of the surrounding residences), while two had low access to services (most services were accessible only by vehicle). The neighborhoods were all between 3,000 and 5,000 in population, and each was served by a single elementary school. Precautions were taken to ensure that access to services was not related to some extraneous fact, such as the percentage of children in the neighborhood, percentage of foreign citizens, population turnover, average income level, or age of the neighborhood. A housing shortage, which existed in Gothenburg until fairly recently, created a situation in which people often had little choice about where they lived. Relatively few families in the study were living either in well-served or in poorly served areas because of personal preference. The study revealed some interesting variations in the way families in different circumstances make use of formal and informal support systems (Tietjen, 1977). Two areas are particularly relevant here: mothers' social networks and families' use of recreational services.

Mothers' Social Networks. Single mothers in the study made greater use of their personal social networks than did married mothers, particularly for assistance in emergencies and for emotional support. They were more indebted to their network members both for practical help (such as borrowing household items and obtaining help with childcare and household tasks) and for emotional support than were married mothers. While there was no difference between married and single mothers in the size of their networks, the relationships reported by single mothers tended to span a greater range of activities. That is, rather than limiting interaction with a particular person to a narrow range of activities, single mothers tended to have more intense relationships that involved everything from socializing to the exchanging of emotional support than did married mothers. Further analysis showed that the somewhat lower socioeconomic status of single rather than married mothers was partly responsible for their greater indebtedness to network members. Apparently the economic hardships associated with single parenthood contribute to greater dependence on friends (than is true of married mothers). These findings reflect the stresses that are inherent in single-parent status, even in Sweden. Interestingly, single mothers are overrepresented among abusing parents in the United States (Gil, 1970), and thus deserve special attention.

Access to services affected the network patterns of married mothers more than those of single mothers. Married mothers tended to have more intense relationships with their network members and to be less indebted to them if they lived in low-service neighborhoods than if they lived in high-service areas. Network patterns of single mothers were unaffected by service accessibility. This finding suggests that the single mothers in the study were making sure their needs were met, whatever the accessibility of services. Regardless of marital status, mothers who lived in neighborhoods with low access to services exchanged more help in emergencies, more frequently shared important information, and provided more emotional support than mothers living in neighborhoods with high access to services.

Swedish services are comprehensive and efficient in providing support to families, but at the time of the study neither informal interaction among users nor user participation was encouraged. By meeting some of the needs of families, formal services may actually reduce the incentive for informal network building. One would expect that families who do not use, or do not have access to, formal family support systems would rely on neighbors and friends more than would families who have easy access to services or who use them extensively. My research showed that this was happening.

Families' Use of Recreational Services. A mother's marital status and type of neighborhood had much less influence on use of formal services than on use of informal support systems. Families living in areas where recreation centers, libraries, bookmobiles, and parks were easily accessible used them more than did families who lived in areas where such services were less accessible. Single mothers made more use of childcare services than did married mothers, reflecting the fact that the single mothers in the study were employed outside the home more often than the married mothers were and so were given priority in obtaining places for their children in the daycare centers. In contrast to families' use of social networks, then, use of services does not seem to be greatly affected by either the mother's marital status or the type of neighborhood lived in, with a few exceptions that reflect the special needs of single mothers for childcare and the kinds of recreational facilities available in the neighborhoods studied.

Relationship Between Use of Services and Social Networks. Three distinct patterns of support system usage emerged from the data. First, those married mothers in neighborhoods with high access to services who made frequent use of services also tend to have large networks, engage in numerous social activities with network members, and have more wide-ranging relationships. For these mothers, then, use of informal support systems and use of formal services are closely related, and both kinds of systems appear to be supportive of these mothers. This pattern may be referred to as supplementary use of formal and informal systems.

Second, for single mothers living in neighborhoods with high access to services, frequent use of services was associated with having small social networks and with engaging in few social activities with network members. This finding suggests that single mothers use either formal or informal support systems, at least for recreation, but not both. From the results reported earlier in this chapter, it appears that single mothers get most of their support from their personal social networks rather than from formal services. The reason for this is not entirely clear, but it may be hypothesized that these single mothers find formal services to be less supportive than informal ones and perhaps less sensitive to or less prepared to deal with the special needs of single mothers. The comments of several mothers in the study about the attitudes of married mothers and about some service personnel they encountered in their dealings with formal services lend strength to this interpretation. The only measure of formal service use that correlated positively with support from informal sources for single mothers in high service areas was attendance at parents' meetings at daycare centers. Otherwise, the pattern of support system use by single mothers may be called compensatory; that is, support from social networks appears to be compensating in a sense for lack of support from formal systems.

For both married and single mothers in areas with low access to services, a third pattern was found. For this group, there were fewer correlations than could be expected by chance alone. It appears that in these quieter, friendlier neighborhoods use of formal and informal systems is influenced less by the nature of available systems than by other, unknown factors —perhaps by the nature of the particular need itself. Thus, my study illustrates the way a family's use of both formal and informal support systems can be shaped by the neighborhood situation and by characteristics of the family itself, even in a society where there is strong cultural support for linking families to both formal and informal support systems. To answer the question of how these links can be built, we can turn to some recent innovations in Swedish social services.

Programs for Neighborhoods

Swedish childcare begins during the mother's pregnancy. More than 90 percent of all expectant mothers are registered at neighborhood-based outpatient maternity clinics (Petersson, 1976). These clinics provide prenatal and postnatal care and counseling for mothers, as well as screening for potential family problems. Every Swedish child is registered at birth with a local child health care clinic. Each clinic serves about 500 preschool children who live in the neighborhood surrounding it. Both maternity care services and child health services are free of charge and available to everyone, and nearly all preschool children are under the continuous care of the clinics. (Once children enter school, their health is checked regularly by school health services.) The clinics provide a variety of services, such as giving regular checkups, providing advice and information on childrearing and nutrition, and screening for physical and behavioral abnormalities. The close contact that clinics maintain with families makes it easy to spot cases of child abuse. When maltreatment occurs, treatment is usually family therapy, a home visitors' program, or, in extreme cases, foster home placement.

In 1976, child health clinics began to experiment with a program of parent education. The general, long-range goals of the program are to ensure that all adults take responsibility for giving all children a good environment to grow up in; all parents receive support in their parenthood and influence over their children's circumstances; and all children and youth are prepared for adulthood and parenthood" ("Föräldrarutbildning: Utdrag Ur Olika Lagarbeten Och Utredningar," 1976, author's translation). The more specific aim of the program is "through group dynamics to activate parents to achieve greater understanding and knowledge about children's needs and behavior and about adult and parent roles, and to make it possible for the parents in the group to support each other and take their own initiative in solving problems" ("Föräldrarutbildning: Utdrag Ur Olika Lagarbeten Och Utredningar," 1976, author's translation).

Parents of newborn infants are invited to attend the meetings in groups of ten couples each. Twelve meetings are scheduled over the first three years of the child's life, and the same couples attend all the meetings together. The meetings are always attended by the head nurse of the clinic, who is a familiar figure to the parents. In addition to the nurse, doctors, dentists, social workers, psychologists, and dieticians may attend and lead discussions on topics related to their areas of specialization. Parents are informed at these meetings about other neighborhood services, such as the daycare center, and they meet the people who work in them. Parents are thus made aware of the formal services available to them at the same time as they are building relationships with each other through group discussions of personal concerns and experiences. One health care center in Gothenburg reported that after one year of the experiment, two thirds of the parents contacted were attending meetings and that the response of these parents to the program was very positive. A government commission has recommended that parent education become part of the regular program at child health care centers and be made available to every new Swedish parent.

Another new program is the so-called open preschool. Parents of children in this program are active participants with the teachers and the children in their daily activities. In addition, parents meet together to exchange experiences and learn about child development. Teachers in the program provide parents with information about neighborhood services and take an active role in encouraging personal contacts among parents. The program helps to build contacts among both children and adults as well as across generations.

A more ambitious effort for building social networks among families is a new method of social work called simply "neighborhood work." Neighborhood work is specifically intended to facilitate the development of personal social networks among residents of a neighborhood. It does so by encouraging individuals to engage in a variety of community projects and events. Projects of this kind have been tried in several Swedish cities and have been well received. This method, which is taught in schools of social work, aims, among other things, to reduce reliance on professionals for the solution of problems and to stimulate a sense of mutual personal responsibility among community residents. There were several neighborhood work projects in operation in Gothenburg at the time I did my research there, and I would like to describe the activities of one especially lively project.

The neighborhood social work project in this particular suburban neighborhood operated out of a ground-floor apartment at one end of the housing area. Staffed by two full-time social workers, the project's stated aim was to create a sense of unity among the residents, to improve contact among children, teenagers, and adults in the area, and to bring about meaningful activities for all age groups. To this end, the project had created an association of residents that elected its own leadership and voted on the activities and business of the association. Some of the activities that had taken place in the project's two-year history were a film program for children, a childcare cooperative, a senior citizens' club, a teenagers' club, a flea market, a crafts program, a neighborhood newspaper, and a full program of summer outings, sports, and crafts that culminated in a party attended by more than 1,000 people at the end of summer. In addition to the main office of the project, which was almost always open and serving coffee, a second large room in the area was used for activities and meetings. The project staff also offered individual guidance when needed and made referrals to appropriate agencies.

There was active and constructive cooperation between the project and other local organizations, especially the parent-teacher association and the nearby recreation center. Both of these were unusually active in this neighborhood and had high rates of participation. Neighborhood residents had worked together in two projects involving agencies outside their area. One of these succeeded in stopping the city's plan to fill in a pond used by local children, and the other involved working with city architects on a plan for an adventure playground to be built in the neighborhood. Accounts of similar projects in other cities (for example, Daun, 1974; Ahlbert and others, 1975) also attest to the success of the neighborhood work approach to building support systems for families. No doubt many readers will recognize their own efforts at community development in this description of neighborhood work.

Conclusion

I have focused on the role of human services in providing formal supports and helping to build informal supports for families. One of my basic themes has been that many different kinds of services—health care, educational, cultural, and recreational—can contribute to the prevention of child maltreatment. They are more likely to be effective in this effort if they are designed and delivered in such a way as to encourage their users to interact with one another and to assume an active, give-and-take role in both formal and informal support systems. I have tried to show how characteristics of society and culture, neighborhood, service agency, and family influence the kind and amount of support that families receive. I have reported on a country where family support systems are in many ways stronger than they are in the United States and where rates of child maltreatment are very low. Finally, I have presented some examples of ways in which service agencies in Sweden have implemented successful programs specifically designed to link families to support systems.

It is impossible to identify a single program, or value, or government policy responsible for the low rates of child maltreatment in Sweden. Perhaps this is the most important and useful conclusion that can be drawn from my analysis. Providing supports for families and protecting children from maltreatment are not simply matters of designing better local programs or of changing attitudes about privacy and violence or even of formulating a coherent national policy on families and children.

Each of these is an important link in the chain, but none of the links is strong enough to do the job alone. Instead, we need to work at all levels if our efforts to support families are to be successful. Sweden has not solved all its social problems, and close emulation of Sweden would not enable us to eliminate ours. It is neither possible nor desirable for us to change our size, our history, our ethnic diversity, or the other things that have contributed to our strengths as well as to our problems. In order to develop and maintain a national sense of competence and control, we need to build on our own values and strengths in solving our problems. Nevertheless, there are some lessons to be learned from Sweden's experience—lessons that could be incorporated, with some modifications, into our own solutions.

Thus, parent education groups such as the ones sponsored by the children's clinics in Sweden or the one described by Benjamin Gottlieb in Chapter Three help parents to become more conscious of their own values and expectations for their children, to become more aware of existing community supports, and to develop their skills in dealing with their children and with other parents. The Swedish children's clinics themselves, which share many of the features of the program described by David Olds in Chapter Eight, are excellent examples of a service that provides support to families at a critical time in the development of the parent-child relationship. The open preschool has the advantage of combating the isolation of children from adults other than their own parents by providing a setting in which groups of parents and children can interact with one another around tasks in which both are building their competence. The "neighborhood work" method, whether adopted in whole or in part, clearly has great potential, perhaps especially for high-risk neighborhoods.

All the programs described here attempt to build the competence of families to solve their problems through interaction with other families and individuals whenever possible. Services that give people the opportunity to participate actively and to interact with one another in the problem-solving process can combine what formal services do best—using their resources and expertise for extraordinary problems—with what is strongest in the informal system—greater breadth, depth, and reciprocity in relationships. But none of these programs can work effectively at the local level in the absence of support from the larger society. The case for a national policy for children and families has been argued powerfully by others (National Academy of Sciences, 1976), and the arguments need not be repeated here. It is clearly futile to hope for a lasting solution to the problem of child maltreatment unless we formulate and enact a national policy that will serve as the basis for a comprehensive network of both formal and informal family support systems.

Looft (1973) has expressed the view that the "model of man" held consciously or unconsciously by policy makers and program designers determines the nature of policy and programs. By defining the options of those who are affected by these policies and programs, this implicit view of human nature becomes a self-fulfilling prophecy. Looft argues that ideas of human nature that declare human beings to be either essentially evil or essentially good fail to consider the role of social experience in forming human beings. There is ample evidence for the existence of both good and evil in human nature. The only useful approach to policy, then, is one that focuses on providing the kinds of conditions and experiences that encourage the development of positive values and behaviors. In seeking solutions to the problem of child maltreatment, we need such a positive approach.

Americans have resisted the idea of a national family policy as being contrary to our most basic values as a nation. But the programs suggested here, along with the policy that would support them, are very much in keeping with some of our most cherished values. We have always had a deep commitment to the integrity of families. In the past, we have chosen to limit the role of the public sector in matters of the family, but this view is becoming less and less tenable as the nature and position of the family undergo rapid and far-reaching changes. We have always had a strong tradition of local control in many matters of government. By building on this tradition in developing support systems for families, we can keep problems of excess bureaucracy and remoteness to a minimum. Helpfulness and neighborliness are two of our most admired national virtues. We can build on them.

Finally, we can make use of the experience of Sweden and other countries for reevaluating our attitude toward making changes in our society. Bronfenbrenner (1976) asks, "How come we can deliver men and survival systems to the moon but we can't deliver health care to the neighborhood? If we're so good at material technology, why not social technology as well?" (p. 26). We have the technology to make change occur, and we have the values to guide us in a wise use of that technology. Commitment and action are what we need now. In the chapters that follow, my colleagues provide strategies for transforming our understanding of how to help into the kinds of actions that are needed.

CHAPTER 3

The Role of Individual and Social Support in Preventing Child Maltreatment

Benjamin H. Gottlieb

When I was invited to prepare a statement about techniques of mobilizing informal social support to address problems of child maltreatment in the community, I had only a nodding acquaintance with research in this area. As a properly trained academic, my first step was to track down the important recent works on the topic. My second step was to go the extra mile and familiarize myself with the history of theories about the problem. However, I believed that my orientation to the area was based not only on book learning. I presumed that I also was informed about the *human* experience of child maltreatment. Some months earlier, I had been working with a student who was interested in studying the interactions among members of Parents Anonymous groups, and I had arranged a meeting with the sponsor of the local chapter to discuss the feasibility of such a project. As it turned out, group sessions had been abandoned because of poor attendance. A telephone service had proven to be much more acceptable locally, as indicated by its high rate of use. When I inquired into the reasons behind parental preferences for anonymous dialogues, I learned a great deal about the life situations of distressed parents—the sparsely populated social world they inhabit, the extreme mood swings they experience, their feelings about themselves and their children, and their pervasive pessimism about their personal futures and the future life course of their families.

With this grounding in the literature and this brief but rich account of several themes common to the lives of distressed parents, I produced an outline of the chapter I would write. But in the interval between writing the outline and drafting the chapter, I radically shifted my perspective on issues of child maltreatment. I experienced firsthand the dilemmas that face a group of residents who are trying to come to terms with instances of neglect in a neighborhood. From this new vantage point, my outline impressed me as a masterpiece of pedantry. It was thick with gray matter and presented in a prose style that would do the most abstract of social philosophers proud. I was spinning a web of prose around constructs, not people. I was plotting hypothetical scenarios instead of coming to grips with the everyday behaviors of people in real settings. And, most important, I was trying to design solutions to problems of my own invention, instead of taking my cues from the parties who would ultimately be asked to implement solutions in their own lives. In short, my ideas were not in touch with the real world. My personal experience led me to a more humble appreciation of what it means to *know* what child maltreatment is all about.

Although my perspective has changed, my purpose remains the same: to describe the variety of informal helping resources available to families in the natural environment. I want to do this, of course, with a special focus on the lives of families at risk for maltreating children. Having adopted the insider's viewpoint, I am now more able to appreciate some of the forces within both the family and the social environment that perpetuate a family's isolation from helping resources. The discussion that follows represents my effort to interlace *ideas* I have about social support with *observations* I have made in the real world.

The change of perspective began after I attended a routine semiannual meeting of my condominium association. The association is composed of twenty-five families who own townhouses and who share responsibility for maintaining the common property on which the homes have been built. Much of our agenda is filled with the mundane business of protecting our joint investment through periodic reviews of our tax assessment, the quality of our municipal services, and the adequacy of our insurance coverage. However, at this particular meeting, another "protection issue" was raised by our president. He reported that several residents were concerned about the safety of our preschool children who played in the private lane that provides access to our driveways. Aside from the natural irritation of drivers who were constantly forced to dodge tricycles and other playground hazards, residents were particularly upset about the behavior of certain children who continued to block the lane despite repeated requests not to. This last statement seemed to electrify the membership, since everyone knew exactly which two children were the guilty parties. A flood of testimonials ensued, beginning with vignettes about the belligerence and rudeness of these children, proceeding to several horror stories about their behavior and appearance, and culminating with a series of inferences about their home life that stopped just short of a total indictment of their parents. There were observations about the childrens' skimpy clothing on cold winter days, their unwashed bodies, and their antisocial or even lewd interactions with other neighborhood preschoolers. Eyewitness accounts gave way to secondhand reports of the disarray in the family's home and the discovery there of a cache of toys belonging to playmates. The inadequacy of supervision was shown by the fact that the children were at times cared for by the eldest daughter, who had not yet reached the minimum age prescribed by child welfare legislation. Finally, the president called for some action to improve the situation.

Although we agreed that local standards were being violated by both parents and children, our responses to the president's call for remedial action reflected a range of essentially punitive measures. At one end of the continuum was the suggestion that we alert the local Children's Aid Society to the possibility of neglect. A dead silence followed this proposal. At the other end was the suggestion that we pen a polite letter to the parents, nudging them to increase their efforts to monitor their children's outside play, but this also received a cool response. Two intermediate solutions were also voiced. One perky mother said that she would have no scruples about approaching the offending parents and "letting them know what we think of the way they're bringing up their kids." And a father, fed up with the obstacle course in our access lane, announced that henceforth he would confiscate any bikes or toys the children left unattended, to be reclaimed by a parent only.

The upshot of this round of suggestions was inaction. We were unable to attain consensus about the most suitable approach. This was tantamount to admitting that none of the suggested tactics was in keeping with the informal bylaws that had developed spontaneously within our little world. We had hoped that just one voice among our group would speak out and say, "Listen, I know Mr. X well enough that I could handle this without causing too much grief," or, "Mrs. X and I often work the same shifts as volunteers in the hospital—I'll see if I can broach the issue at work." But the fact was that none of us had an ongoing relationship with either parent. Nor did we participate with either in any common settings that might provide an opportunity for the formation of personal ties. Indeed, although we lived in physical proximity to these people, we inhabited separate social worlds. And, without a common and trusted messenger who was relatively permanent in the lives of both parties, we sensed that our message would be heard as a threat and would only widen the gap between us. In short, we could not invoke the informal bylaws that sustain social life in our neighborhood since we could find no acceptable point of entry to these two neighbors.

Our present immobility stood in sharp relief to past experience. We were accustomed to greeting new neighbors upon their arrival. Our formal organization helped to quickly establish a norm of social responsibility for common concerns, and this norm extended easily into more personal domains. For example, three families had banded together for the purpose of securing good daycare for their preschoolers, and several fathers had organized a car pool to work. My own toddler attends the same nursery program as the daughter of another neighbor, and we have not only swapped lunch invitations but we have listened to one another's "pet peeves" about the kids' behavior. We try to be consistent in implementing each other's disciplinary regimens when we supervise the children. Aside from such conspicuous forms of informal social support, there are many routine practices that enhance our sense of security about our neighborhood and make everyday life less taxing. Most of us feel that we can count on one another to keep an eye on the house when we leave for extended periods, and it is a common practice to pass the house key to the next-door neighbor to ensure that plants and pipes survive our absence. In the winter, it is expected that we will inform one another of the arrival of the snow removal service, so that no one will be stuck with a blocked driveway because a car has not been moved.

These are examples of the kinds of practical services that commonly are exchanged among members of our neighborhood-based support system, but informal social support can take a variety of other forms within basic or primary group helping networks. And here, I would like to depart briefly from the particular scenario that has unfolded in my neighborhood to present a more comprehensive description of the ways in which lay people define the substance of informal support. My understanding of this matter is based in part on a study I conducted among single mothers that resulted in a classification of twenty-six kinds of helping behaviors. Details about the procedure I used in that study are presented elsewhere (Gottlieb, 1978). My purpose here is to present some of the salient features of informal helping that I discovered in my study.

The Substance of Informal Support

In my research, I found that mothers who are the sole support for their families receive four kinds of help from people. The first type, which I called "emotionally sustaining" help, includes several helping behaviors that make it easier for people to explore their problems by providing them with a safe, supportive context. Most of these behaviors are part of good therapeutic technique for counselors (Carkhuff and Berenson, 1967), and several of them are at the heart of what Goodman (1972) has called "companionship therapy." They also reflect the importance of simple contact with a trusted party during stressful episodes and thus are antidotes for social isolation. The second type of help, which I called "problem-solving behaviors," includes ways of helping that augment the mother's own problem-solving resources by providing new information, new ideas, or direct assistance. The third type of help involves indirect forms of assistance, including simple availability ("unconditional access") and a willingness to make resources available without hesitation ("readiness to act"). Each of these indirect ways of helping describes an important aspect of the environment's reliability as perceived by the women in my study. The fourth type of help is "advocacy." It occurs when the helper takes steps to reduce a problem at its source by intervening on another's behalf with some important people or group. A prime example of this involved a neighbor who helped a mother by speaking to her landlord about waiving a damage deposit. (In Chapters Six and Seven, Diane Pancoast and Alice Collins describe how this kind of helper can be an important bridge between formal and informal support systems.)

Returning now to my experience with the problem in my own neighborhood and generalizing from it, I will briefy summarize the social conditions that often prevail when neighborhood residents find themselves unable to intervene in situations of suspected child maltreatment. At the start, people observe repeated instances of children's misbehavior. They notice the youngsters' generally neglected appearance and the absence of adequate parental supervision. Although these people may suspect that child neglect is occurring, they do not take remedial measures for two main reasons. First, the responsibility for taking action is diffused throughout the community, since everyone thinks that some other neighbor has an ongoing relationship with the parents and could call on that rapport to initiate changes. People assume that the family is linked to a local natural support network through someone else. The second reason for inaction is the reverse of the first. People adhere to broad cultural norms that prohibit intruding into other people's privacy, and they are more likely to consider themselves intruders when they see themselves as outsiders. But there comes a point, if the problem persists or intensifies, when the outsiders recognize that social support has not spontaneously arisen or that it has not been effective. At that stage, the outsiders must meet together, formally or informally, and achieve a common definition of the situation as one that requires intervention. In short, the outsiders need social support from each other or from a third party before they can mobilize themselves to act.

In my own neighborhood, we did in fact reach this latter stage, that is, we drew on social support for the decision to intervene. However, while we all agreed on the need for action and on the message we wished to deliver, we were stymied for lack of an acceptable messenger. In other words, we felt that the message would have its greatest impact if delivered by a party who was trusted and valued by the target family. What we sensed from our lay perspective, in fact, has been extensively documented in research literature on the significance and usefulness of primary group attachments in the lives of people. Evidence of the crucial role that valued peers play in counteracting a diversity of stressful experiences bolsters my conviction that primary group support also can be an effective resource in addressing problems of child maltreatment.

Types of Social Support that Can Reduce Stress

Primary Group Ties. The literature on this subject includes both anecdotal and experimental evidence spanning the fields of social psychology, epidemiology, sociology, and social work, as well as laboratory research on animals exposed to a variety of stresses. These latter studies usually conform to the following pattern: Animals are exposed to some sort of stress—for example, an electric shock or crowding. Some of the animals are exposed to the stress in the presence of others of the same species, and some are exposed to the same stress alone. When attachments exist between the animals, symptoms of stress do not appear (Cassel, 1974).

It is hard to ignore the parallels between these findings and those situations in which people have benefited from the presence of others who shared common attributes or experiences. Such effects have been documented among women coping with life changes associated with menopause (Coelho, Hamburg, and Adams, 1974), among adolescents making the transition from high school to the first year of college (Hamburg and Adams, 1967), and among patients recovering from severe injuries (Coelho, Hamburg, and Adams, 1974). Eitinger's (1964) observations of Nazi concentration camp inmates led him to conclude that those who lived with another family member or maintained contact with prewar friends were able to cope more effectively with the camp experience in the long run than were inmates without such attachments. Norwegian ex-inmates testified that "being together with other Norwegians" was the factor that contributed most to their survival. When people share something important, they can handle life's challenges much more effectively than would otherwise be true.

No doubt many who are familiar with recent developments in the human services field will immediately make the connection between these studies and the contemporary proliferation of self-help groups (Gartner and Riessman, 1977). In fact, the "active ingredients" in both are the same. The difference is that, when people join mutual aid groups, they often are strangers. They do come to identify with one another very quickly, however, and are encouraged to associate with one another outside group sessions. This tactic further accelerates their incorporation into one another's "personal communities." Certainly, the exponential growth of Parents Anonymous as a coping resource among persons who feel that they are prone to child maltreatment indicates that this organization is seen as an attractive and probably more acceptable forum for problem solving than professional agencies of change. A recent independent evaluation of the impact of Parents Anonymous groups (Behavior Associates, 1977; Lieber and Baker, 1977) adds scientific credence to past personal testimony of its members.

Hard data are also accumulating from a series of studies that contrast the health of people who are enmeshed in an informal support network with the health of those who are isolated from interpersonal supports. For example, French (1973) has looked at social support in the work setting. He altered numerous aspects of job stress, such as workload and role ambiguity, in an effort to assess whether social support on the job prevents individual strain under these conditions. Generally, he has found a reduction of strain in socially supportive situations, as measured by a variety of blood-trace tests. Another study (Burke and Weir, 1977) looked at the effect of a strong helping relationship between husbands and wives on their perception of "well-being." The results of this study revealed a strong direct association between helping and well-being. A third important study tracing the healthy effects of primary group bonds was conducted among women in their first pregnancy (Nuckolls, Cassel, and Kaplan, 1972). That study found that, among women who had experienced relatively high levels of stress both before and during their pregnancies, those with numerous "psychosocial assets" had only one third as many complications as women with few such assets. In short, those with supportive social bonds were less susceptible to the negative by-products of stress. These rigorous studies, considered alongside laboratory findings and the impressions of participants in mutual aid groups, provide consistent evidence for the importance of social bonding in moderating the effects of stress. Moreover, they all have a direct bearing on the problem of child maltreatment.

Community Gatekeepers. To this point, I have focused my attention on the importance of family members and close associates who may buffer individuals against the adverse effects of stress. But kith and kin do not exhaust the kinds of friendly contacts potentially available for vulnerable families. There is much evidence that those persons commonly referred to as "community gatekeepers" can have a helpful impact on others' lives. Here, I am referring to citizens whose work roles bring them into regular contact with the public. These are people who come to be trusted and who are often in a position to observe and deal with the buildup of tensions.

A number of large-scale surveys have shown the high frequency with which people turn to representatives of the health, educational, religious, and legal institutions for help in resolving emotional turmoil (Gurin, Veroff, and Feld, 1960; Ryan, 1969; Rosenblatt and Mayer, 1972). Yet, despite the fact that family physicians, clergymen, teachers, and the police do field the concerns of so many people, it is probably safe to assume that these gatekeepers, like their psychiatrically trained counterparts, tend to serve only those citizens whose social styles match those of the gatekeepers themselves. There are, no doubt, many people who are uncomfortable in bureaucratic surroundings, who feel disadvantaged relative to the gatekeeper's credentials, and who feel estranged from anyone who is part of an agency that in their minds exists to provide social control, not social support. For example, in a study I conducted among four subgroups of adolescent youth (Gottlieb, 1975), I found that the group perceived by classmates as socially deviant did not have access to the helping resources of the school staff. In contrast, those adolescents belonging to subcultures that conformed to the school's mold of the "ideal citizen and student" were rewarded with the personal attentions and help of the school's gatekeepers.

Among people outside the milieu of community gatekeepers, another type of informal helper may be more accessible and more effective. Here, I am referring to such neighborhood figures as bartenders, cabdrivers, local merchants, and hairdressers. They, too, maintain sustained contact with local residents, can offer emotional support and practical aid, and can help close the social gap between many low-income people and community gatekeepers. While Diane Pancoast's chapter on the role played by "natural helpers" describes one type of such resources, E. L. Cowen and others (1978) have probed aspects of the helping relationships maintained among a sample of ninety hairdressers in Rochester, New York. In that study, an average of one third of the time that a hairdresser spent with a steady customer was taken up by talk about the client's "moderate to serious" personal problems. The matters most frequently discussed included, in order of importance, problems and concerns about children, physical health, marital problems, depressive feelings, and common anxieties. Another impressive indication that these beauticians were acting as informal helping agents is the fact that the majority had received calls for assistance outside "office hours" and had been visited in their homes by clients for the purpose of further discussion of their clients' problems. In considering the study's implications for future planning of helping services, the authors conclude: "Exact knowledge of de facto help-giving mechanisms is an essential precondition for upgrading society's total help-giving effort. The precise forms that such upgrading might take cannot yet be divined. One possible change, however, is a reallocation of professional time away from direct, after-the-fact restorative services toward roles that strengthen the frontline contributions of natural support systems and informal caregivers. Beyond the reality that such a reorientation would address, it could also lead to a geometric expansion of effective help giving in ways that might cut down the flow of later, serious problems—precisely those in which professionals, with at best limited success, have always been asked to engage" (E. L. Cowen and others, p. 18).

This exhortation to professionals to engage in activities that will tap the potential of natural support networks brings us full circle to my own backyard. Social networks are at the heart of the matter. I have tried to lay the groundwork for a discussion of the types of resources that can be mobilized through and by a person's social network. At this point, I want to talk specifically about such networks.

Social Networks

The idea of social networks takes into account the sources of informal support that I have reviewed, since family members, friends, community gatekeepers, and informal caregivers (such as beauticians) can all be viewed as prospective members of a family's social network. Thus, in its most inclusive sense, the social network represents the set of all persons with whom one interacts. Sociologists and anthropologists have used social networks as a way to analyze social structures (Laumann, 1973). Sometimes authors focus only on people's "effective networks" (Epstein, 1961), restricting their analyses to those close associates with whom the focal person interacts most intensely and regularly and who are regarded as social peers. But this restricted view is not suited to our purposes, since we may wish to assess a given family's connections to community gatekeepers who, though not considered social equals, may be persons who are trusted and accepted sources of help.

To illustrate the main features of the social network as a tool for assessing a family's social environment, I have drawn a figure composed of a series of concentric circles surrounding the family unit (Figure 1). The nuclear family occupies the innermost circle, while the adjacent ring is occupied by family members and close friends, people who can be described as primary group helpers. The succeeding rings are inhabited by informal caregivers and community gatekeepers, while professional helping agents occupy the outer ring, a position that reflects their distance from the interior, everyday world of the family. There are other ways of sketching social networks (see, for example, Barnes, 1975), but I have adopted this format both because it builds on my earlier classification of primary group helpers and because it highlights the fact that many families are insulated from these potential supports in the environment. I am arguing that avenues into family life will be achieved only after a period of intensive reconnaissance in the social networks of families. We need to know about the range of community settings in which a family participates before we can learn about the people whom the family trusts and find out who are sources of parental support, as well as who can be mobilized as agents to change the family. Then, in turn, we must learn something about the culture of these trusted people—the parenting norms to which they subscribe and their propensity to bend their tal-

Figure 1. A Family and Its Social Resources

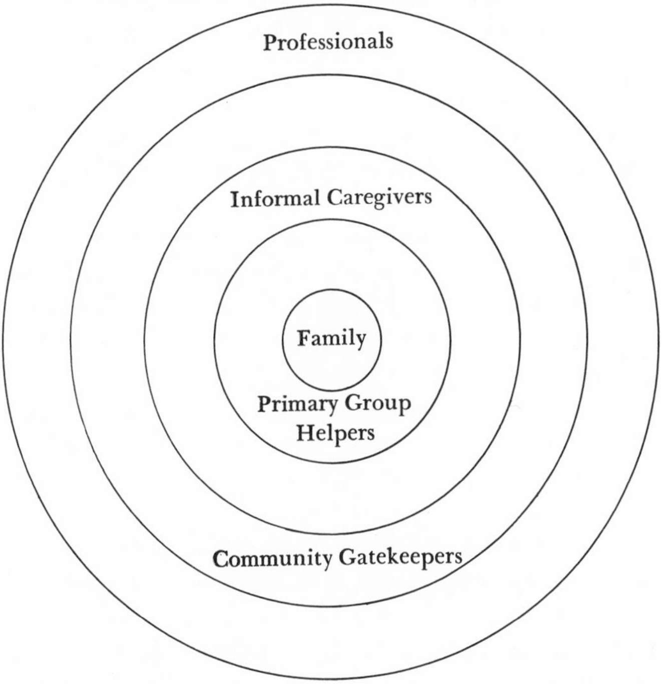

ents toward helping parents reexamine and redirect their parental behaviors. In many cases, we may find that families formerly described as "hard to reach" are now accessible, but only when approached by members of their own social network on their own "turf." In other cases, we may find that the family is virtually isolated from supportive social attachments and that new openings to the outside must be made. In fact, there is much evidence that child maltreatment occurs most frequently among families encapsulated in a ring of privacy so thick that it functions as a barricade against the "normal" outside social world (Garbarino, 1977b). Here the task is to penetrate this barricade—a task that requires examining and modifying the forces within the family that maintain the wall and at the same time finding openings to outside resources.

Impediments to Formation of Supportive Social Ties

Turning first to a consideration of family problems that may block the development of relationships with external helping resources, it is conceivable that:

- Family members *lack the skills* necessary to maintain supportive relationships.
- Family members *participate in few social situations* so that there is little opportunity to form supportive relationships.
- Family members are overburdened by the demands of everyday living to the point that there is *no time* to develop personal attachments.
- Family members *subscribe to the norm of self-reliance* in matters pertaining to the management of stress, particularly stress relating to the parenting role.

Any one of these problems can harden the boundary between the family and potential sources of support in its environment. I will comment briefly on each of these problems, consider how it may apply to the family in my own neighborhood, and suggest strategies for overcoming each source of resistance.

Without the requisite affiliative skills, social isolation is inevitable. I am not referring to the kind of social skills associated with peak performance in a singles' bar or a bingo parlor, but to skills in initiating and maintaining intimate and continuing personal ties. I am talking about such behaviors as listening, cooperating, considering the other person's perspective and needs, and conducting oneself in a manner that conveys respect and esteem for him or her. People who cut others off all the time, make constant demands for attention, and rarely reciprocate or disclose anything about themselves simply don't make good friends. They are not the sort to whom even a beautician could be attentive for very long.

In addressing this problem, I think first of the need for improved early childhood education, with the accent on training to increase both children's motives to affiliate and their affiliative skills. I then think of the variety of training packages currently available that cover everything from assertiveness skills to child management, including a program to train persons in helping skills (Danish and Hauer, 1973). But neither of these solutions seems practical for families who are isolated and mistreating children *right now*. Early childhood education represents a reasonable primary preventive strategy for laying down the roots of caring and helping relationships. But training programs require a "carrot" or a "stick" to prompt participation on the part of isolated families. Thus, despite the availability of a "technology" for transferring affiliative skills, a skills training approach cannot be implemented except through the friendly auspices of someone who is trusted by the family. In fact, there is some evidence that clients are most effectively recruited to participate in family life education programs when personal and face-to-face strategies rather than mass media campaigns are used. For example, one recent study conducted for the Family Service Association of America (Beck, Tileston, and Kesten, 1977) concludes that "successful recruitment of nonwhite families probably requires *in-person* rather than *phone* contact" (p. 10).

There is little doubt that much of my neighbors' concern about the misbehavior of the newcomers' children stemmed from the fear that their own children would suffer from such poor examples. The new children knew little about sharing toys, cleaning up, and speaking politely. They clearly did not share local values about affiliating, and they suffered the consequences: parents eventually forbade their own children to initiate play with "the new kids" and turned them away when they called at the door. In short, lacking affiliative skills, these children, like their parents, became marginal members of their local peer group. Furthermore, as we have already noted, the parents were viewed as inaccessible for the purpose of correcting their children's behavior, much less for the purpose of enrolling in a program to improve their own parenting skills.

To the extent that people participate in few community activities, they are exposed to a limited range of social resources. If people possess the skills necessary to form social relationships, they can profit from the experiences and varied perspectives of others. Even in the absence of such skills, however, participation in social settings provides an opportunity to observe how others deal with personal problems and to notice that others are experiencing problems similar to one's own. Indeed, the simple recognition that others are "in the same boat" can normalize one's own situation and trigger the motive to affiliate with them (Schachter, 1959).

In any community there are many settings in which interactions between adults and children can be observed. These settings range from such formal ones as the classroom to totally informal ones, such as neighborhood playgrounds where parents can mix easily, especially if they see one another on repeated occasions and their children become acquainted. Other settings include fast-food outlets, YMCAs, and youth clubs whose survival depends upon parental participation. Parents can also observe one another's child-centered interactions in such settings as cooperative preschools, nursery programs, or play groups. In these, parents often rotate as supervisors and, since none qualifies as an expert, there is little apprehension about being evaluated. My point is that participation in a diversity of settings in which there is opportunity to observe the stream of behavior between parents and children allows parents to obtain indirect feedback about their own style, relief about what they may have viewed as unique troubles, and incentive to affiliate with peers. Conversely, if parents do not venture outside their family's own confines or participate in only one or two outside settings where they see other parents, there is little chance that their current practices will change.

How do we go about the task of tying people to multiple settings in the community? I think we need to ensure that those settings are not perceived as threatening or stigmatizing, as being "owned" by an elite group, or worse, as involving efforts at social reform. I am referring to settings that are both *in* the neighborhood and *of* the neighborhood so that people do not feel self-conscious about being in them and can slip easily into the activities that take place. But even if such settings were created and had absolutely no barriers to admission, I think that many families would still be reluctant to take the initial step and would require a face-to-face invitation. In extending the invitation, one should emphasize, first, that the invitation is motivated out of a need for help and, second, that only a small commitment is being sought. For example, the invitation might be phrased, "We need a linesman to stand in for Mr. Jones this Sunday at the kids' soccer game in the park, and I wondered if you could spare some time," as opposed to making a request that would require an indefinite commitment, involve intense personal interactions, and draw upon a special skill. In short, although the ultimate goal may be to move people's self-perceptions to the point where they define themselves as "joiners," this is predicated upon a series of small requests (Freedman and Fraser, 1966).

Finally, certain groups in the community have little mobility across settings through no personal lack of inclination. People who receive government assistance (sole-support mothers, for example) are discouraged from enrolling themselves or their children in many community programs not only because of prohibitive costs and unfavorable community sentiment but also because of the written and unwritten welfare regulations governing their lives. Such regulations include the policy of refusing daycare subsidies to single mothers who are receiving government benefits and are enrolled in postsecondary education, as well as the policy of financially penalizing such women for working outside the home. Welfare recipients are expected to stay at home much of the time, and their petitions to enter vocational training or engage in volunteer work often are met with the accusation that they are not satisfied with their lot. These policies—and the attitudes that go along with them—represent additional instances in which the current social welfare system acts as a way of controlling people. Such policies and attitudes reinforce social isolation and a state of dependency on bureaucracies rather than fostering social participation and social support.

Returning to the case of our new neighbors, it appeared that neither parents nor children participated in any voluntary organizations or clubs in the community. The four-year-old was not enrolled in any of the preschool programs such as the cooperative nursery that my own three-year-old attended or the story hour at the public library. Instead, the family chose a more individualistic or private form of daycare for their preschooler, placing him in the care of an older, widowed woman who lives outside our residential area. Nor did their seven-year-old participate in the pre-Cub Scout program or any of the soccer and hockey teams set up to serve this age group. Furthermore, there were good reasons why the father did not form associations locally. He was not only occupied by the demands placed on the owner of a large manufacturing business—demands that included frequent and extended travel—but the plant itself was located some fifty miles from his home, forcing him to adopt a commuter's schedule. Hence, even if he had been motivated to join local associations, it is doubtful that he could have attended regularly, much less have honored the obligations associated with many of our community service clubs that sponsor youth activities. Consequently, the job of chaperoning children to their extracurricular activities fell upon the mother, who was preoccupied with an academic regimen. In short, both parents had committed major blocks of time to a set of activities that had little to do with their parenting roles and had invested themselves so thoroughly in these settings that they were virtually unable to engage in compensatory child-centered activities. They did not have or refused to find enough time to take good care of their children.

The few hours following the children's bedtimes may present opportunities for participation in voluntary organizations, but not of the sort that involve parent *and* child. Furthermore, weekend and evening hours may be given over to rest and recuperation, or at best they may be devoted to "time out" for the parents to reestablish communication with each other following a week absorbed in private concerns. Although this family's situation anticipates my next point—that considerations of available time may limit parental participation in community activities—many parents with a certain amount of free time may still have inaccurate perceptions of the demands that community organizations will place on them, or they may have fears about a mismatch between their own styles of living and those of the participants in such organizations.

As an illustration of how an outreach program can be designed to link families to new attachments in the community in a way that is not threatening, I will summarize the main elements of a program we have initiated locally. Our program, which is similar to ones launched in Sweden, is being conducted in collaboration with three local family physicians. These physicians are convening parent support groups composed of eight to ten couples drawn from each of their practices. The couples are randomly selected instead of being chosen on the basis of their vulnerability. Since the emphasis is on primary prevention, there is no stigma associated with participation. Furthermore, the physician is drawing upon his relationship with the family to solicit their participation. The sessions will continue over an eight-week period, meeting one evening per week and rotating from home to home. The first session will be held in the physician's own home, and his wife will also participate throughout. In this way, we are attempting to reduce the social distance between patient and physician, while promoting affiliation among the parents.

Although the physicians will offer medical information where appropriate and will distribute some educational material about child development, nutrition, and parent-child interactions, the focus is on the parents' own needs. We want to create a situation in which people can comfortably share experiences and, as the process of social comparison unfolds, can obtain both direct and indirect feedback about their own norms, behaviors, and feelings as parents. The only structured exercise we will incorporate is the periodic use of one-to-one discussions to encourage the formation of close interpersonal ties. We hope to expand the participants' repertoires of problem-solving behaviors that can be used when stressful family situations arise. We will also encourage members to contact one another between sessions to discuss both positive and negative events that arise during this interval. We have even toyed with the idea of setting up a "buddy system" to expedite these exchanges.

In sum, this program capitalizes on an existing prosocial contact, the friendly auspices of the family physician, to create a setting in which social comparisons among peers can heighten the motive to affiliate, culminating in the creation of new attachments. Ultimately, the program's success hinges upon this final step, over which we have no control. We can engineer a social climate that will encourage the formation of interpersonal bonds, but we cannot manufacture human attachments.

Families that are overburdened by the demands of everyday life simply do not have the time or energy to cultivate relationships that support the parental role and/or the family unit. Especially in single-parent families or families in which both parents work, the activities that go into maintaining the home, the children, and the job can occupy a seven-day week. What leisure time there is can be filled more easily by television than by other people, especially if those other people are perceived as equally harried and tired. And in families where a premium is placed upon a few hours of home-based relaxation, serious measures may be taken to defend that leisure time against the demands or even the needs of children. Given the finite amount of energy available, external social attachments are unlikely to evolve so long as daily stresses continue and leisure activities revolve around the home.

An opposite pattern, involving a high level of participation in civic life, may not generate support for the family either. Parents who immerse themselves in community life by joining country clubs, taking active roles in unions and service clubs, and donating time to a variety of volunteer activities may be satisfying important personal needs for social competence and recognition, but this pattern of high participation may have the same effect as its opposite if none of these settings provides the kinds of feedback and support that bear upon family life and parental competence. In short, the quantity of participation in community life is less important than the quality of the relationships that are formed in the process. And one important qualitative measure is the extent to which the parties provide one another with support and feedback. Here, intervention must focus on changing the pattern of everyday life. Parents who continually overextend themselves, either in the world of work or in civic life, and who do not in the process form ties that sustain family life are risking physical and emotional damage to the family unit. A situation of "familial hypertension" evolves that is analogous to medical hypertension. The individual engages in an unhealthy life-style reflected in an excess of work, poor nutrition, lack of exercise, and insufficient rest. This pattern takes its toll physically and emotionally, and its effects can be reversed only through a total change of life-style. Like the hypertensive individual who is confronted with such a global recommendation by his physician, the hypertensive family must reconsider its priorities and establish a new equilibrium that reflects these priorities. Relationships that support the family must be built into this new regimen of living in order to monitor compliance and to facilitate future family development.

While the preceding paragraph places responsibility for change on the family itself and emphasizes in particular the need for the parents to reexamine their values and priorities, a case can be made that the community should take the lead in enhancing family support. Daycare programs ought to extend into the evening hours, thus providing time for the parents to go out or just some quiet time for them at home. Financial barriers to good childcare ought to be removed. Flexible work hours should be introduced on a wide basis to allow more time for the entire family to be together during daylight hours. Aside from their annual United Way checks, local employers could make an important contribution to community social services and youth programs by allowing their employees to substitute "community service" for several of their regular work hours. Some employers already do this and more should join them. Such policies would encourage family involvement in external social settings and maximize the possibilities of forming the kinds of social ties that support healthy family life.

The formation of ties to helping resources can be blocked by values that mandate self-help, not mutual help, as the appropriate recourse for all ills. A "bootstrap" philosophy may be ingrained so deeply that even signs and symptoms of family distress are concealed. Here again, if existing members of the family's social network also subscribe to the idea of rugged individualism, those who do observe the buildup of family tensions are unlikely to openly acknowledge it or take action. The family is, after all, one of the few remaining private affairs in a world in which the government and a host of lawyers exercise increasing control over people's lives. But social isolation is one of the costs of this cherished privacy. One way to deal with this situation is to extend the value we place on sharing and reciprocity to include people's emotional lives. Just as we now think it appropriate to borrow a cup of sugar, we can invent ways to make it possible for people to borrow help in handling life's routine ups and downs. Of course, many of us do this already, so in a way we are trying to reinvent the wheel. But people who don't naturally take part in this kind of emotional sharing need to be brought into new social settings where they can have contact with new reference groups that will offer acceptance and a sense of belonging. Social support is predicated upon these social conditions. The people that a family trusts and who are also sources of parental support can be mobilized as agents of change on behalf of the family.

Conclusion

I have noted four problems that may perpetuate the social isolation of families. They represent forces inside families that build and maintain walls against the outside world and its potentially supportive social resources. I have also suggested how one might go about reducing this internal resistance. Drawing on my own observations of one family in my neighborhood, I have attempted to illustrate how a deficit in the affiliative skills of the children, combined with the family's lack of integration into the broader community, resulted in its virtual isolation from the natural support systems that already existed. These considerations also help to clarify our understanding of my fellow residents' inability to locate a messenger who could effectively communicate our informal bylaws to the offending family and assist the parents in improving the situation. We felt intuitively that any efforts we made, as strangers, to forge openings into the family would be met with resistance as strong as that expressed toward remote professionals or community gatekeepers who are socially distant.

Although this example has helped me to appreciate the conditions that perpetuated this family's isolation, my understanding is limited by a lack of information about many other aspects of the family's social network. For example, I have said nothing about this family's kinship ties, a potentially critical source of support. However, even here we must be careful *not* to assume that we can best advance through the auspices of existing extended kin, since we may be stymied for some of the same reasons associated with the family's own isolation. These relatives may also hold values that isolate them. They, too, may be overburdened and lack helping skills. We cannot blindly proceed on the assumption that family and community ties radiate positive consequences in all the potentially difficult aspects of life. Some people and their social groups need substantial direct assistance and must change important patterns in their day-to-day lives if they are to provide adequate childcare.

Finally, our discussion of this family and its relationships with the rest of the social world will be incomplete unless we return to consider how this family came to be seen as deviant in the first place. Throughout this chapter, I have proceeded on the assumption that the parents were neglecting their children or at least were at risk for doing so. My neighborhood shapes my definition of acceptable family behavior. It determines my threshold for tolerating deviance, and it has also created certain informal channels for getting things done in the area. The point is that in another neighborhood this family might still be socially isolated, but all the other families might be too. In still another neighborhood these parents might perceive their neighbors as similar to themselves and take the initiative in forming associations. Affiliative styles might be well matched and attitudes might be congruent. In such an area, we could not rely on the neighborhood to identify neglect, let alone respond to it. Before we can count on the neighborhood to help families, we must know something about it—who lives there and how it works. If we are always "strangers," we run the risk of misunderstanding the world of families as it exists in the neighborhood. The following chapter is devoted to a discussion of these issues. It attempts to distinguish different types of neighborhoods from one another and to describe the values and networks of support associated with each.

CHAPTER 4

Support Systems in Different Types of Neighborhoods

Donald I. Warren

The last few years have seen a resurgence of interest in neighborhoods. Researchers, human service professionals, and others have begun to realize that neighborhoods are often an important link in the chain between the family and society. In some cases, the potential for preventing and creating child abuse and neglect differs from one neighborhood to another. For example, in some neighborhoods it may be hard to find out whether there is maltreatment or whether such cases as do exist are being dealt with effectively. In other areas, neighbors may be eager allies for professionals who are seeking information to help parents

Note: The author would like to thank the National Institute of Mental Health and the Center for the Study of Metropolitan Problems, which funded the work on which this chapter is based.

61

care for their children. In this chapter, I will introduce some ideas that have grown out of my earlier research into neighborhoods (Warren and Warren, 1977). Specifically, I will discuss ways of defining and analyzing neighborhoods, their functions for individuals and families, and their organizational structures. Then, drawing on my research on neighborhoods in Detroit, I will discuss six types of neighborhood settings that may be found in a metropolitan area. Finally, I will briefly examine the implications of these different neighborhod types for mobilizing support systems on behalf of families.

Neighborhoods as Social Structures

Before we can examine types of neighborhoods, we need to focus on the meaning of the term *neighborhood*. Are neighborhoods defined mainly or solely by geographical boundaries? In some studies, high school districts are said to be neighborhoods. In other studies, an acknowledged subcommunity such as Greenwich Village is termed a neighborhood. One study employs the following working definition of neighborhood: "A family dwelling unit and the ten family dwelling units most accessible to it" (Caplow and Forman, 1950, p. 360). In a study of Israeli ethnic groups (Shuval, 1956), a "microneighborhood" is defined as one composed of three families—the respondent's and those of his two closest neighbors. Another researcher uses this same definition in speaking of a "nuclear neighborhood." Yet another investigator (Greer, 1956) sees the problem of the size of the neighborhood unit in terms of four social units: (1) household, (2) neighborhood, (3) local area of residence, and (4) municipality; this researcher describes each unit as performing distinct social functions.

While these all are reasonable ways to identify a neighborhood, none is totally adequate. Confusion about what a neighborhood is results from three factors: (1) the size of a neighborhood unit is confused with its social closeness; (2) assumptions are made about a neighborhood unit without first separating out the accidental elements that are irrelevant to its essential character; and (3) there is a failure to define the role of "neighborhood" when traditional "natural areas" (that is, those with homogeneous populations, strong social traditions, and so forth) have broken down because of rapid social change. The very definition of the term *neighborhood* is often grounded in the subjective. A neighborhood is that through which an individual experiences society—first as a child, later as a parent, and still later as a retired person. Morris and Hess (1975) put it this way: "When people then say 'my neighborhood,' it usually means they have found a place to live where they feel some human sense of belonging, some human sense of being *part* of a society, no matter how small, rather than just being *in* a society, no matter how large" (p. 1).

Yet there is obviously an objective side to neighborhoods, too—the availability of city services, the upkeep of houses and alleys, the congestion or openness of the area, the style of housing, and the way these influence neighborly exchanges or inhibit them. My own research in the Detroit metropolitan area used the elementary school district as a starting point for defining neighborhood. Urban and suburban elementary school districts usually have a population of several hundred families and a total population averaging between 2,500 and 5,000 persons. Central to the notion of the elementary school district is the concept of "walking distance" for the child. Such a basis of neighborhood was also selected by Morris and Hess in their book *Neighborhood Power* (1975): "What is the neighborhood? It is place and it is people. It has no defined size or even scale, although commonsense limits do appear throughout history. The homeliest tests for neighborhood would include the fact that a person can easily walk its boundaries. It is not so large that going from one side to another requires special effort. Its physical size means that it is or can be familiar turf for everyone in it" (p. 6).

So a neighborhood is both an image in the minds of those living there or hearing about an area by reputation and the resources and physical dimensions that characterize it. As we try to understand the human potential of neighborhoods, we must keep in mind this sometimes complex combination of factors. A group or a neighborhood is more real than its members may recognize for the very reason that it has its own established social values, roles, and patterns of acting. In this sense, it is more than its own geography. It is what social scientists describe as a "social system" or "social structure."

Neighborhood Functions

As a social structure, the neighborhood may perform a diversity of functions for its residents. It may act as an arena for informal interaction, a center for interpersonal influence, a source for mutual aid, an organizational base for formal and informal organizations, a reference group, or a status arena. Not every neighborhood performs all these functions, of course. Some neighborhoods may be very effective in performing some functions, but quite ineffective in performing others. The extent to which each of these functions is carried out in a given neighborhood, however, has implications for the development, identification, response, and eventual treatment of families involved in child maltreatment.

An Arena for Informal Interaction. When a neighborhood functions as an arena for informal interaction among residents, it can be said to be high in "neighborhood sociability." Sociability between neighbors usually manifests itself in "back-fence" exchanges. It serves to mitigate some of the depersonalizing influences of the urban environment and often provides a sense of social belonging for individuals. In this sense it may serve as one of the support systems for families discussed in Chapter Two. Here is the way this characteristic is described by one resident who participated in the Detroit area research: "I was out there trimming the tree, you know. And Manny was out there fertilizing his lawn. First thing you know, he was offering me this saw of his and I was trimming everything in sight. The neighbors across the way saw us and we got to talking about the time Jessie fell off the ladder and Tom [yet another neighbor] drove him to the hospital to have his sprained ankle taped up. But, you know, things are like that around here. You get to talking about one thing and pretty soon we're on each other's porches drinking beer and shootin' the breeze." Such a willingness to exchange greetings provides the opportunity for further interaction.

A Center for Interpersonal Influence. Although neighborhoods serve as important arenas of sociability for the individual, they also function as centers of influence, both overt and subtle. The focus of influence may range from the way one decorates a kitchen or landscapes a yard to methods of child-rearing and voting preferences.

What begins as aid in a simple home improvement can sometimes result in more far-reaching socialization, as witnessed in the following example taken from an interviewer's notes:

> We were particularly interested in the Larkin family because they moved in as we began our ethnography. They were so different from the rest of the neighborhood. Not in the way they looked but the way they acted. You have to understand that this neighborhood has a fantastically involved parent group and groups of preteens, teens, and so forth organized for explicit mutual aid purposes. Behavior is so damned rational.
>
> When the Larkins moved in, we noted in our conversations that there was yelling—child yelling at child, parent at parent, and all combinations. Talking with that family (and with their neighbors) this year was a real trip. The kids were all on various teams, and the parents had been given parties as new residents and asked to join other groups. They [the parents] declined, but other neighbors took it upon themselves to have the Larkins over, to invite them to monthly block clubs. Anyway, you wouldn't recognize this as the same family. The atmosphere actually begins to approach rationality.

Through the process of continuous observation of the behavior of neighbors, "learning by imitation" occurs. This learning frequently involves neighborhood peer groups of both adults and children.

A Source for Mutual Aid. Exchange of help among those living in close proximity in urban areas is another frequent and important function of neighborhoods. Such help includes emer-

gencies as well as daily crises. It means exchanging goods and
services of various kinds, and it may be as simple as borrowing
the proverbial cup of sugar. The following field notes from the
Detroit research provide examples:

> I really don't socialize with my neighbors
> much, but you know you can count on them.
> There is the sense that if something happened, they
> would be there. One kind of thing is if somebody
> gets a load of gravel or a load of dirt they are going
> to put on your yard, everybody will come over and
> sort of throw in a hand.
>
> Or with a friend, if you come home and you
> just bought some beer but it's hot, you might send
> a kid down with the hot beer and trade it for some
> cold beer. Or if you run out of sugar. But it
> wouldn't be like a regular kind of thing. You
> would replace the sugar . . . maybe a beer or some-
> thing, but the exchange may be generalized over a
> long term.

Not only can neighborhoods substitute for external support but they also can insulate residents against outside intru-
sions. For example, after the 1967 riots in Detroit, residents of
black neighborhoods helped each other by refusing to give information about their neighbors to bill collectors. Similarly,
resistance to discussing or reporting maltreatment can be part of
"mutual aid."

An Organizational Base. People living in a given locale
may be "joiners" of many groups. But a critical question to be
asked of any neighborhood is whether it has block clubs, PTAs,
or other local organizations that are for the neighborhood
and are used by it. If a neighborhood has these groups, it functions as a political and organizational base. Neighborhood participation may (1) parallel participation in wider circles of the
community, (2) compete with other social units in the community, or (3) link with, and facilitate participation in, the
larger community. In one study, Fellin and Litwak (1963)
found that for individuals who are trying to raise their social-

class standing, participation in the local community may serve as a basis for moving up and out of the neighborhood. Other research offers evidence that voluntary associations help to speed the integration of individuals into the local neighborhood.

A Reference Group. The saying "home is where the heart is" can often be applied to the neighborhood. The neighborhood can be a "comfortable" place. It can be a basis of identity, a place filled with people to whom one feels a degree of commitment. In sociological terms, it can function as a "reference group." Individuals may be guided and changed in their behavior and values as a result of what they understand to be the social norms of their neighbors. In his general review of the nature of neighborhoods, Mann (1970) refers to expectations in a social milieu "where a person feels that people around him think and act as he does" (p. 76). Mann argues that a neighborhood resident "has expectations of a similar outlook on life amongst his neighbors, particularly insofar as life in the neighborhood itself is concerned. So if people want to go out from the neighborhood to work in other parts of the city, if they want to spend their leisure time in the city center, these things do not particularly matter *unless* in some way they affect the neighborhood" (p. 581).

The social climate of a neighborhood may lead individuals to seek out others in an area who they think will agree with them and, therefore, will reinforce attitudes they already hold. But merely believing that a majority of one's neighbors agree with you may have the same effect. This "pluralistic ignorance" may be facilitated by the very lack of extensive social interaction that makes the urban neighborhood something less than an intimate primary group setting.

A Status Arena. There is yet another kind of activity that can go on in a neighborhood, even in a neighborhood where there is not much communication between neighbors. It involves the way people furnish their houses, the kinds of cars they own, and the other means they use to express status, individuality, and economic achievement. A neighborhood may act as a mirror of personal achievement and well-being in two basic ways. First, the neighborhood may screen out definitions of

class or status that are valued in the larger society but that have
no relevance at the local level, while simultaneously serving as a
source of status claims that replace those valued by the larger
society. Thus, in a blue-collar neighborhood with little variation
in income or types of housing, craftsmanship may become a
status element, with the highest status accorded to that family
able to build the most elaborate addition to its home. The second and more obvious manner in which the neighborhood may
mirror personal achievement is by providing an arena within
which status claims derived from the larger society can be
"cashed in" in terms of housing, a life-style emphasizing con-
sumption, or some other highly visible definitions of social position. The more elaborate the stonework or brick on the exterior
of a home, the more expensive the automobile or fencing, the
more individuals appear to have "made it" in our society.

Neighborhoods differ not only in the extent to which
they perform certain functions but in their organization as well.
Some are highly formalized and hierarchically structured units
that might better be called miniature bureaucracies. In such settings, people have fixed roles. They know who the leaders and
the followers are. They know who specializes in fixing fences
and who can help when people are feeling depressed or have
sudden illnesses or need someone to look after their houses
when they are gone. Most neighborhoods, however, are less
structured. Still others are too weak even to restrain violent behavior or enforce any kinds of social norms.

But no matter how they are organized, all neighborhoods
can be expected to possess some individuals who assume special
roles as problem solvers. These individuals may be of several
types:

- *Officers of Local Organizations:* These officers represent
  formal leadership to which they have been elected or ap-
  pointed. Such individuals often have other informal leadership roles, but their basic legitimacy comes from the block
  club, PTA, or other organization in which they serve.
- *Opinion Leaders:* These individuals may be "back-fence"
  helpers or specialists in some capacity. They typically are ap-

proached for advice or information about a particular problem. Such people may offer help and advice or give information about where to get further help. As norm setters and "referral agents," they usually are not part of a formal group.

- *Neighborhood Activists:* These people have reputations for getting things done but are not necessarily members of organizations. Some neighborhoods have many of these individuals. In some cases one activist knows another, and there is cooperation between them. In other instances, each activist has his or her own sphere of influence. Activists often have no formal roles. Even when they do, their "leadership" legitimacy is a function of reputation, not of structural position. Neighborhood activists may exist in any type of neighborhood. When understood in terms of the functional and structural fabric of their particular neighborhood, activists can become critical resources in the development of strategies to combat child abuse and neglect.

Types of Neighborhoods

In my research, I assessed geographic neighborhoods by examining them along three social dimensions:

1. *Identity:* How much do people feel they belong to a neighborhood and share a common destiny with others?
2. *Interaction:* How often and with what number of neighbors do people interact on the average during the year?
3. *Linkages:* What are the linkages to the larger community? Are there people who have memberships in outside groups or bring news about the larger community back into the neighborhood?

These three factors are among the most critical for understanding how neighborhoods work and, therefore, for understanding the different situations in which people find themselves when they want to take action at the neighborhood level. Taken together, these elements constitute the *social-structural characteristics*—that is, differences in organization—that cut across social class, income, or ethnic lines in our society to define what neighborhoods really are for people in urban areas.

Eight basic types of neighborhoods can be constructed by assigning high and low scores on each of the three underlying key dimensions. Six of these types (integral, parochial, diffuse, stepping-stone, transitory, and anomic) represent the most frequently occurring forms. Two other types are logically possible, but they appear far less often than the other six forms. Table 1 compares the six major types.

Table 1. Different Types of Neighborhoods

Type	Identity	Interaction	Linkages
Integral A cosmopolitan as well as a local center. Individuals are in close contact and they share many concerns. They participate in activities of the larger community.	+	+	+
Parochial A neighborhood having a strong ethnic identity or homogeneous character. Self-contained and independent of larger community, it has ways to screen out what does not conform to its own norms.	+	+	−
Diffuse A homogeneous setting ranging from a new subdivision to an inner city housing project. Residents have many things in common. However, there is no active internal life or ties to the larger community.	+	−	−
Stepping-Stone An active neighborhood resembling a game of "musical chairs." People participate in neighborhood activities *not* because they identify with the neighborhood, but often to "get ahead" in a career or some other nonlocal point of destination.	−	+	+

(continued on next page)

Table 1 *(Continued)*

Type	Identity	Interaction	Linkages
Transitory A neighborhood where population change has been or is occurring. It often breaks up into little clusters of people. Frequently "oldtimers" and newcomers are separated, and there is little collective action or organization.	—	—	+
Anomic A nonneighborhood that is highly atomized and has no cohesion, with great social distance between people. There are no protective barriers to outside influences, making it responsive to some outside change, but it lacks the capacity to mobilize for common action from within.	—	—	—

The Integral Neighborhood. This type of area points in two directions at once. People in this type of setting are cohesive. They know each other, interact with each other, and belong to a lot of organizations—block clubs, PTAs, and so forth. They are very active in the neighborhood itself. But an integral neighborhood also fits in and meshes with other institutions in the larger community. It has an effective base organization. An integral neighborhood often has a large number of professional people who are involved in community, business, political, and civic work. A thorough knowledge of their neighborhood automatically affords them access to the social control agencies of the community.

An integral neighborhood can accomplish some rather special things. When a problem comes up, its residents can reach out to various organizations. If there is someone in the neighborhood who is on the board of directors of a corporation, for example, he or she can deal with a problem that neighbors are experiencing and deal with it very quickly. This kind of neighborhood is also able to identify local problems, get a group going, and really take action to solve them. Its activities are both internal and external. People who belong to neighborhood groups also belong to groups that are not in the neighborhood. Hence, it is a cosmopolitan neighborhood as well as a local center.

The integral neighborhood may be one of the most important "inventions" of the modern urban environment. While it is usually easier for higher status groups to create such a neighborhood, it in fact occurs in widely different settings. Here are three examples of its ubiquitous possibilities, excerpted from field research notes:

> *A White-Collar Neighborhood.* Most of the organizational structure is at the larger community level, the city level, and it reaches down into the neighborhood. You can see it manifested in the neighborhood in that you can talk with people who are participants in organizations, churches, PTA. Some of them (like PTA, Girl Scouts, Cub Scouts) have local counterparts. They are part of a larger organization, but they have an entity at the local level. But most of the organizations are at the community level, and they just have members who reside in the neighborhood. So in that sense it is not autonomous at all. I didn't find any organizations in the neighborhood that were exclusively neighborhood based. Ties in and identification with the larger community are very great.
>
> *An Inner City Neighborhood.* I assumed that urban renewal would have a negative effect since it draws attention to dilapidated areas. I learned otherwise. The school system has a reputation for having one of the very best elementary school areas and a very strong PTA. There are several community leaders, some of the key leaders of the whole city who appear to elevate the neighborhood's status just by virtue of the fact that they live there. There is definitely a positive reputation. It has a reputation outside as an old area with a core of really good people and a fine school system. I got the sense that it was sort of looked to with the

respect of an old area that had gone through a transition but was still in there. Some people I talked to had fond memories of the neighborhood since their parents used to live there.

A Blue-Collar Industrial Neighborhood. Ford Park is . . . like a small town. The people who were active in citywide organizations lived in neighborhoods with people who were involved in local organizations. These citywide groups had connections to various organizations that were local to Ford Park, so people were involved in the same organizations together. The neighborhoods were very important to these organizations. There was more collective scheduling when everyone was free from the factory. Their emphasis was on nonwork activity, encouraging organizations, social clubs, and the like.

In the integral neighborhood there are a large number of activists who are linked to one another and are very task oriented. While they may have close working ties with local groups on occasion, they form a rather distinctive stratum whose major function is to provide linkage with external groups. They are less visible in the neighborhood as compared to the leaders of the elaborate associational structure of the neighborhood, but their presence is often felt in the neighborhood's political activities. They are a stable feature of the neighborhood's leadership structure and rarely use militant direct action tactics.

The Parochial Neighborhood. In this kind of locale, we have a version of the traditional neighborhood toward which so much nostalgia is directed. There often is a strong sense of ethnic identity within the area—a sense of homogeneous values and culture—along with the whole panorama of ideas that have long been associated with the cohesive local community or neighborhood. (I am using the word *parochial* in its nonsectarian sense. The connotation is that of a self-contained world.) This is a neighborhood with values that often run counter to those of the larger community. It does not draw its values from outside. It is not a consumer of values so much as a producer of values. As such, it at times may appear to be deviant or out of line with major values of the larger society. For example, it is not likely to be a locus of strong support for women's liberation, school busing, or liberal policies.

When it relates to the larger world around it, the parochial neighborhood uses a significant degree of insulation. The barrier is sometimes linguistic, sometimes organizational. The area may offer a set of solutions that duplicate what is found in the larger community and thus provide very effectively for the needs of its residents without having to resort to the "outside" society. In that sense, this is a very self-contained community. It also tends to be very protective of its values, possessing a set of "controls" that provide for the enforcement of those values.

The parochial neighborhood often has a basis for group identity that allows it to sustain its uniqueness fairly easily. This basis may be racial, occupational, or generational. Here is how people in parochial neighborhoods describe their locale in response to the question, "What things do you like best about living here?"

> Our neighbors are friendly, kind, generous with their time—helping with kids, giving of themselves when needed. It is kind of secluded down here, so we don't have door-to-door salesmen (male, age fifty-eight).
> Like I said before, I like the large lots. That's why I came over here. . . . I like most of my neighbors—not all of them but most of them. Just about everything you need is close by, even the gas station (female, age forty-nine).
> Neighbors have concern for each other which you do not find in a big city. It is close here. The neighbors have to be close to each other mainly because we are all black. You know I am not going to tell on my brother. We have to stick together (male, age thirty-six).

One example of a parochial neighborhood, as described in field research notes, is an area of modest income families located at the edge of Detroit. This urban neighborhood has grown from a farming village to a carriage and trolley town and then to a white neighborhood in a black worker's city. Its fine system of social services, its hospital and local city hall are all part of the larger city but retain a distinctly local character. It is an ethnic neighborhood where the stress is on being American. Its wealth relative to the rest of the city gives it some political leverage, but its residents are not traditionally activists and feel exploited by the more intellectually liberal and active segments of the city. Many residents grew up in a provincial atmosphere of a small town never seeing the center of the city. In a city that survives in large part on welfare, these neighborhoods are fiercely independent even if eligible for aid.

In the parochial neighborhood, media information—whether about health, childrearing, or other significant events—seldom passes directly into the neighborhood. Whatever information does get through is filtered and modified by key "opinion leaders." These individuals usually have very strong commitments to the neighborhood, and they are not likely to express to their neighbors the interests of the larger community. On the contrary, they are more likely to circulate the neighborhood's own concerns among its members. "Activists" in parochial neighborhoods tend to protect the neighborhood against outside influences that are not consistent with neighborhood norms, while, at the same time, communicating news of what is happening in the outside world.

The Diffuse Neighborhood. Far more common than the parochial neighborhood is what we describe as the diffuse neighborhood. Often highly selective in its recruitment of residents, the diffuse neighborhood tends to provide a rather homogeneous setting (for example, subdivisions in suburban areas or public housing projects in urban locations) and to offer a situation where many families move in at about the same time. What distinguishes the diffuse neighborhood from the parochial neighborhood is that the former has almost no active life of its own. Diffuse neighborhoods have potential for collective action, but they don't exercise it. As an example, consider a fairly affluent suburban neighborhood in which people are all in middle-level management. If you went from door to door, you would find remarkably similar values and outlooks, but these similarities simply exist—they haven't been locally generated. It is not critical to the life-style and needs of the people that they act together as a community.

In the diffuse neighborhood, people achieve a degree of consensus without interaction. So limited is the interaction, in fact, that people may not even be aware of this consensus. For example, researchers found in one such neighborhood in Detroit that virtually all residents interviewed brought up an article on "privatism" that had appeared in the paper. Their thinking was similar on many crucial issues. Along several blocks in the same neighborhood, however, the backyard shrubs had died because of the fumes and traffic from nearby parking lots. Each person griped, but none realized that neighbors shared this concern until the researchers mentioned it.

In a diffuse setting, people don't need the neighborhood. They don't depend on it for helping behaviors, and their own social networks are not focused on the neighborhood. People identify with the neighborhood because they find it a pleasant place to live. In this situation, information often flows very slowly, with the result that people may perceive higher (or lower) agreement on issues than may, in fact, exist. Consequently, the neighborhood is often relatively slow in taking action when threatened. On those occasions when the neighborhood is galvanized into taking action, residents learn a new sense of solidarity and engage in increased interaction. However, this newfound activism is usually short-lived, subsiding back to its normal level in relatively little time. Thus, only under conditions of crisis or threat does this kind of neighborhood become organizationally active.

In diffuse neighborhoods, neighborhood activists are relatively autonomous leaders who have ties to the external community and whose motivation is based on their desire for numerous social contacts. Usually they find their greatest satisfaction in working with outside groups, and what actions they do take in the neighborhood tend to reflect their own priorities and interests in linkage with these outside groups rather than to be expressions of effective neighborhood organization. On those occasions when they do try to respond to the requests of residents, they rarely get very far. This suggests that there is very little exchange of information in the neighborhood. The activist has to go to almost every household if he or she wishes to make individual contact.

The Stepping-Stone Neighborhood. In contrast to the diffuse area, we have the neighborhood whose outstanding feature is that people don't identify with it but nevertheless perform various important functions within it. We call this a stepping-stone neighborhood. It is marked by a paradoxically high degree of activism, even though there is a large turnover in residents. A typical stepping-stone neighborhood may have a large concentration of highly mobile, lower-level executives who come into the area, very quickly join all the organizations and become leaders of the neighborhood groups, and then, two years later, move on. The pattern of organization in the community is somewhat like that of musical chairs. That is, a lot of new people are coming in and out of the neighborhood and participating in its activities, but their ultimate commitment is not to the neighborhood but to their careers or to some other goals. Such neighborhoods institutionalize this kind of turnover, adapting well to the constant change in leadership. The people are talented and leadership oriented. They like their neighborhood, but not too many stay. They usually move when the number of children becomes too large for the home. For these people, a larger home means a higher status. People move here to get away from integration in other parts of the city and feel a greater sense of belonging to their churches than they do to any neighborhood groups.

Stepping-stone neighborhoods are found in many social groups. They represent what Vance Packard (1972) sees as the new living pattern of mobile, rootless Americans. My own research shows this kind of neighborhood to be an increasing phenomenon, especially at the fringe of urban centers. One neighborhood staff observer put it this way in her report: "Temporariness is a paradox in a sense because, on the one hand, high status is shown by improving your home, and, on the other hand, the people move from these homes, into which they have put so much, into higher-status areas. Perhaps the way to move to a higher-status area is to come from one that gives a reasonable amount of status in itself—or at least one in which the status criteria haven't changed in a while so it can be specifically, with reasonable accuracy, defined."

The stepping-stone neighborhood is not the most typical kind of area, but it is of particular interest owing to the paradoxes it embodies. It is somewhat like the integral neighborhood in that it has a degree of internal organization that is matched by the outward focus of many of its residents, but the population itself presents a different profile. The pattern of mobility generally stems from the many individuals who move in to be close to their place of occupation but who are called upon to move again, either up the ladder or laterally, as soon as the organization or corporation changes its needs. In this kind of neighborhood, people are very active in outside organizations. Those who are neighborhood activists usually achieve this role in subordination to their participation in larger community groups. Thus, if individuals who move into a neighborhood are officers in outside groups, they may quickly become neighborhood activists and establish links to the residents of their neighborhood. The neighborhood leader does not rely on successful communication *within* the neighborhood. Rather, the leader relies on leadership skills from outside organizations. In the stepping-stone neighborhood, the activist is often in training to become a member of the larger community's political elite and he or she uses the neighborhood activist role as a preparation for that elite status.

In keeping with its dynamic character, many kinds of action tactics may be tried in a stepping-stone neighborhood. A willingness to engage in direct confrontation is not lacking. Although the neighborhood may have a high turnover of such leaders, it appears that activists are an easily "renewable" leadership resource. Highly motivated to play their catalytic roles and primarily "social-emotional" in leadership style, they use tactics that bring them in contact with newcomers as well as with oldtime residents. Yet they also have many ties to outside organizations. In a number of ways they serve as a strong force for expressing the needs and interests of the neighborhood to external organizations and to those who have a less involved organizational life but who are local residents.

The Transitory Neighborhood. In the transitory neighborhood, the population turnover is so great and/or the institutional fabric so divided that there is very little collective effort. There are no institutions at all for dealing with this situation. In contrast to the stepping-stone neighborhood, where newcomers are immediately swallowed up by the organizations, there is little activity in the transitory neighborhood, and what activity there is often breaks down into a series of cliques. These little clusters of people sometimes last for decades. Individuals belong to the same groups and never allow newcomers to "join." Since newcomers to such neighborhoods participate very little and oldtimers a lot, there is very little agreement on issues, as well as a lack of neighborhood cohesion. Here is an almost classic instance of the transitory neighborhood as described by one interviewer:

> Usually [neighbors] just say hello to each other and maintain [only the] most basic relationships. When asked why, most of them will reply that they or their neighbors just moved in or that they plan to move out of the area soon so that they did not have a chance or do not think it is worth it to start more intense relationships. The neighborhood is apparently of a transient, highly dynamic nature, and most of the residents feel it is not worthy of a "larger social investment." The newcomers are uncertain as to whether they are wanted, and the old residents do not know how to "start talking" to new people, especially if they are black and "shy."
>
> But, even the race is not [entirely] to blame for the fact that somebody is [treated as] new on the block. Sometimes people live together for years and do not know each other at all. Someone told me about a recent event to illustrate this phe-

nomenon: One evening, inhabitants of a residential street could hear a woman screaming for help from a house and no one but a stranger, a black man who was passing by, answered her cries. Several minutes later he went up and down the street asking neighbors whether someone knew the woman and could stay with her in the house. To his surprise, no one admitted knowing and no one went in to help! (She had been living on that street for many years, and she was white just as her neighbors were.) Hence, he went back and stayed with the woman until the ambulance came and took her and her husband (who was actually the cause of the panic) to a hospital.

This story really tells something about the lack of neighborhood feeling or human interaction and about the almost paranoid fear and suspicion among people in the area.

In such a neighborhood, one avoids participation in local entanglements either because the new families moving in tend to be different from oneself or because the very diversity of the neighborhood makes it difficult to feel any common set of values with one's neighbors. The absence or decline of local cohesion in the transitory neighborhood means that activists and more formal leaders often are dominated by ties to outside social networks. Under conditions of population turnover or clique formation, quite diverse sets of individuals tend to exert pressure on these outside networks, often with highly competitive tactics and goals. Too often, activists in the transitory neighborhood are lone entrepreneurs who can be militant and effective in expressing neighborhood concerns but who do so on behalf of a constituency that is sometimes more historical than current, more a clique than a cross section of the neighborhood. In transitory neighborhoods, the primary task is to broaden and/or strengthen neighborhood organizations.

The Anomic Neighborhood. We come now to what is virtually a "nonneighborhood," that is, the anomic or individuated neighborhood. Here, people simply go their own ways. They don't belong to organizations. They may not see much of each other at all, and they have all the usual symptoms of members of a mass society. In short, the neighborhood is not a focal point of community. In anomic neighborhoods, moreover, we find virtually no leadership structure. Whatever linkage occurs with outside organizations does not really flow through any neighborhood activist system. Even groups that meet in the neighborhood do not really possess any neighborhood identity. Therefore, leadership and the role of the activist involve nothing more than the obligations and tasks that an individual might take on as a single resident or as a representative of some group to which he or she belongs. There are no meaningful constituencies for the person who is active, and there is no real cohesion to the structure of influence. Individuals may choose to live in the anomic neighborhood in order to have the kind of anonymity that they consider necessary for their own life-styles. But the fact remains that the anomic neighborhood cannot readily mobilize to respond to common interests.

The anomic neighborhood should not, however, be seen as a neighborhood that cannot respond to change. As a matter of fact, what people may not like about it is that it is unable to resist change. The anomic neighborhood is not uniquely identified with low-income areas either. It cuts across social strata and can be found in the suburban housing project or condominium. Wherever located, however, the anomic neighborhood sets up barriers between neighbors. Here is an example in one such area in relation to personal hostility and crime problems:

> There are a lot of individual hassles. Their children get into fights or problems. After they clear it up, the parents continue to feud. That is still on an individual basis. There is [some] indication that when these feuds take place they are not really long-lasting, permanent things. . . . The Jones are on the blacklist this week. Next week it might be the Smiths and the Jones will be OK again. . . . The church has been robbed at least once. . . . It has five or six buses. They are constantly siphoned. Windows are broken in the buses. . . . There is the

neighborhood fence. Frank's Bar and Lounge was
robbed. The car wash is where they distribute the
drugs. And then there is the one house that has been
robbed three times, and a couple of other homes
have been broken into.

There is a lot of crime there for such a small
area. People talk about it, but they don't talk
about it in terms of what shall we do about it; they
just talk about it to note the fact. You get the feeling that people think, "Well it hasn't happened to
me so I don't really give a damn. When it happens
to me, I will be concerned." We know at least one
person that works closely with one of the detectives on the drug squad. She's worked with her
family . . . and her son. Her son is involved and she
wants to deal with it. But you get this noncommittal,
noninvolvement.

Research in the Detroit metropolitan area suggests that between
one fourth to one third of all neighborhoods in that city fall
into the anomic pattern.

Problem-Solving Capacities of Neighborhoods

The typology of neighborhoods provides a basis for comparing the general problem-solving capacities of local areas. In
assessing such capacities, we must take into account the following factors:

• *Problem definition*—the subjective meaning that a given situation has for members of the community. Is the problem perceived as natural or artificial? Short term or chronic? Subject
to change or fixed? How do residents view the need to respond when the problem is posed by the larger society and
imposed on the local population? Do they resist imposed controls or regulations, develop insulating mechanisms, and selec-
tively receive and attend to mass media messages?
• *Mobilization*—the ability of a local community to interact
quickly, to contact agencies, to obtain information and com-

municate needs, and so forth. Often the very nature of the problem requires speed, as in the event of sudden illness or accident or of a meeting called on short notice.

- *Saturation*—the extent to which messages from the media reverberate throughout local informal networks and cliques. Is the finding of a unique approach to coping with a problem widely shared by all members of the local community? Innovativeness in response and diffusion of such approaches tend to go hand in hand and can be compared between communities.

- *Maintenance*—the ability of a community to sustain its newly generated response to a problem and the social mechanisms that can reduce deviance and increase conformity to the goal. Some communities may have excellent resources for helping to meet a short-term emergency but very limited ways to sustain longer-term, less dramatic needs of individuals and the total community.

In Table 2, the general problem-solving capacity of each of the six major neighborhood types is summarized. Each of these local community settings can be seen as having some capacity to facilitate, resist, or institute change. In some cases, they are innovative and generate new values. In other cases, they are able to protect existing values. And in still other situations, they are able to receive new ideas and influences.

Table 2. General Problem-Solving Capacities
in Six Neighborhood Types

Integral Neighborhoods	High potential for response to goals generated by the larger society due to low alienation; rapid institutionalization of problem-solving behaviors; rapid diffusion of media-derived and locally derived information; rapid response and capacity for maintenance of appropriate behaviors.
Parochial Neighborhoods	Low potential for response to goals generated by larger society due to high alienation; rapid institutionalization of problem-solving behaviors; rapid diffusion of locally derived information; rapid response and high capacity for maintenance of normatively supported behaviors.

Table 2 *(Continued)*

Diffuse Neighborhoods	Slow diffusion and response to problems in initial phase; discrepancy between attitudes and behavior can be quite high with social control mechanisms for responding to externally generated goals limited largely to value agreement and homogeneity of population; maintenance is moderately high once initial behavior is institutionalized.
Stepping-Stone Neighborhoods	Response to problems often very rapid, with newcomers to the area quickly socialized to respond to local norms—norms often derived from the larger society and brought into the local context; uneven diffusion and high population turnover that may weaken ultimate level of problem response.
Transitory Neighborhoods	Low identity with the local area leading to reliance on external information and agencies of social control or the breakdown of such mechanisms; splits between newcomers and oldtimers reduce diffusion; conflict over norms and limited mobilization of social control slow initial reactions and limit sustained responses.
Anomic Neighborhoods	Absence of coherent value systems limits initial speed of response (either positive or negative); presence of individual responses but little diffusion; moderately effective external control processes and information interventions.

The response that individuals make to a problem within their neighborhood can be viewed as a three-stage process: (1) identification or recognition of a problem (problem identification), (2) informal efforts to solve the problem (problem coping), (3) and actions to involve formal helping agencies outside the neighborhood (problem externalization). In this section, I will describe these three stages, briefly showing how neighborhood types differ in the extent to which their residents go through them.

Problem Identification. Identification of a problem such as child maltreatment depends on the nature of the family's perception of its own behavior and on how others define the problem. It is a self/other labeling process. In the integral neighborhood, visibility of all family behavior is likely to be high, and behavior that deviates from the norms of the neighborhood will be subject to some attempt at change or control. Here we are speaking of the probability that a neighbor will notice a deviant behavior pattern or call it to the attention of others in the neighborhood. By contrast, the anomic neighborhood will be unlikely to have norms about "deviant" behavior. Or, if such norms do exist, visibility will be low and mechanisms for transmitting their meanings to others in the neighborhood will be nonexistent.

In a parochial neighborhood, a great deal of the response to parental behavior in the identification phase will depend on the norms about childrearing. Behavior that is consistent with these norms will usually find acceptance. If it is inconsistent, rejection will be similar to that within the integral neighborhood. In both the diffuse and stepping-stone neighborhoods, the visibility and rejection of deviant behavior will be moderate, but for different reasons. In the diffuse neighborhood, people interact relatively infrequently, although they often share common social values. In the stepping-stone neighborhood, recognition is given to those who are active in organizations and who share the values of the "joiners." The difference between newcomers and oldtimers is not the key issue; rather, the fact that organizations change members frequently and do not really take in all residents becomes the deciding factor. In the case of the transitory neighborhood, the mechanisms of participation have declined, and there is little opportunity for interaction. Thus, visibility is restricted to the most immediate neighborhood or is uneven throughout the total area. Rejection of behavior that deviates from larger societal norms is theoretically present but in fact is not mobilized.

Problem Coping. In this second stage of problem solving, neighbors may help each other directly or may refer a person with a childrearing problem to someone in the area who can be of help. Referral at this point would be only to helpers within a network of primary group contacts. As can be seen in Table 3, the probability of an attempt at direct help or referral differs markedly by neighborhood type. In the integral neighborhood, for example, many helping resources, from skilled individuals to specific local groups, can be tapped, and the probability of direct

Table 3. Stages of Problem Solving in Six Neighborhood Types

Neighborhood Type	Problem Identification		Problem Coping		Problem Externalization	
	Recognition of Deviant Behavior	Rejection of Deviant Behavior	Helping	Helper Referral	Readiness to Report Local Problems to Professional Agencies	Readiness to Use Professional Agencies to Solve Problems
Integral	High	High	High	Medium	Medium	High
Parochial	High	High to Low	High	Medium	Low	Low
Diffuse	Medium	Medium	Medium	High	Medium	Low
Stepping-Stone	Medium	Medium	Medium	Medium	High	High
Transitory	Medium	Low	Low	Medium	Medium	Medium
Anomic	Low	Low	Low	Low	Medium	High

help is therefore high. The same is true in the parochial neighborhood. However, for the diffuse neighborhood, helping networks within the neighborhood itself are limited. Thus, referrals to friends or resources outside the neighborhood may occur at a higher rate in the diffuse than in either the integral or parochial neighborhood. In the transitory neighborhood, a similar but even more extreme pattern prevails. Local resources are very limited, and, consequently, contact with a network that includes outside persons is also restricted.

Problem Externalization. In the third problem-solving stage—externalization—neighbors may report a problem to a formal institution or seek help from such an institution. The neighborhood that is least likely to report problems and that has the most ability through normative controls to prevent its residents from engaging in a particular behavior is the parochial area. By contrast, the stepping-stone neighborhood has high contact within the area and is oriented to the larger society, and so is the most likely of all neighborhoods to report to the police or other agencies any problems that its residents feel are not being adequately handled informally. Table 3 also shows that the integral neighborhood resembles the stepping-stone and anomic neighborhoods in its readiness to actually use outside community agencies. In the integral area, the problem that must ultimately be dealt with by outside agencies is one that has already been "handled" by local informal processes. Thus, in the integral neighborhood, high readiness to use formal services does not imply high actual use. In the anomic and transitory neighborhoods, high and medium readiness to reach out to formal agencies implies that such contact occurs for a wide range of problems that might have been successfully handled by informal helping structures had they surfaced in other kinds of neighborhoods. Thus, the input from anomic and transitory neighborhoods to community agencies is liable to be excessively high and to limit the desire and ability of such agencies to seek further outreach to these locales.

Problem-Solving Pathways

In each type of neighborhood, an individual resident is likely to use or to have access to several "problem-solving pathways"—that is, sets of community resources that he or she may tap to solve a particular problem. Which pathway an individual ultimately selects is to some extent a function of the person's abilities, knowledge, and previous experiences. But it is also a function of available resources and the structural context in which he or she seeks help or is given help. Thus, what an agency does (its administrative style, the role patterns of its staff, and the means it uses to reach out into the community), along with how an individual reacts to or anticipates professionals, affects his or her choice of agency.

Typically, preferred or "model" patterns of help seeking can be identified for each neighborhood context. These are ideal types from which actual behavior may deviate, but they form clusters that reflect the social structures of neighborhoods. These "pathways" can be summarized as follows:

· *Full System Utilization Pathway (integral neighborhood).* In this model, both lay and professional systems are integrated and draw upon the unique capabilities of each when appropriate. Here the lay system is seen as both a legitimate adjunct and an alternative to professional service. Use is made of lay, quasi-institutional, and formal service systems in problem coping.

· *Indigenous Resource Pathway (parochial neighborhood).* This model is characterized by a population with a rich set of supportive social relations. This population prefers such relations, for a variety of social and cultural reasons, to professional help sources. Residents make use of lay and quasi-institutional systems that are in close physical proximity and are insulated from formal service systems by social *and* physical distance.

· *Nonindigenous Resource Pathway (diffuse neighborhood).* This pattern is one in which individuals are in close contact with friends, family, or other lay helpers who do not live in the local neighborhood. Quasi-institutional helpers are utilized often in the work setting or in church or other settings. Formal agencies, where contacted, are not linked to the local area. Local resources are underdeveloped, often because other systems are easily available or because people use friends, relatives, and other lay helpers outside the area.

- *Ricochet Pathway (stepping-stone neighborhood)*. In a stepping-stone neighborhood, the pattern varies with the population group and may be characterized by "full system utilization" or by a "ricochet" pattern. In the latter instance, a population may be relying on quasi-institutional and lay resources not necessarily out of preference, but because of difficulties in making use of the human services system. This may be due to the great difficulties of overcoming social, normative, or cultural barriers. Or it may be due to the unwillingness of professional agencies to deal with particular problems or problem definitions, especially of the more "settled" or "inactive" members of a given locale.

- *Autonomous Routing Pathway (transitory neighborhood)*. The "autonomous routing" or "plug-in" model illustrates a situation probably characteristic of a population that is highly informed about professional resources and that has few people on whom to rely in the natural setting. Even here, though, large and important differences can be expected between populations.

- *Dependency Relationship Pathway (anomic neighborhood)*. This model is one in which the person becomes enmeshed or "trapped" in the network of professional agency referrals or becomes "captured" by an agency that views him as a particularly desirable client; that is, he shows progress, is compliant, and is easy to work with. Here the professional agency expands into the client's "life space."

To put the analysis of neighborhood problem solving on a less abstract level, let me now show how the residents of two neighborhoods differ in attempting to solve the problem of child abuse and neglect. The neighborhoods in question are contiguous, white, working-class neighborhoods in the older section of a suburban city. While outwardly similar (that is, they have some similar demographic, socioeconomic, and ecological dimensions), the neighborhoods fall into two different neighborhood types—the parochial and the anomic.

A Parochial Neighborhood. The first neighborhood fits

into our classification of a parochial neighborhood because of its homogeneity of values and culture. To illustrate the types of social interactions and helping networks found in a parochial neighborhood, we have included the following excerpts from an ethnographer's field notes on this neighborhood:

> Child abuse is cared for within the neighbor-
> hood, as everyone crisscrossing the organizational
> boundaries feels a sense of responsibility toward *all*
> neighborhood children, and child abuse represents
> a clear breach of neighborhood norms. Since many
> of the neighborhood voluntary organizations deal
> with children as target populations, problems are
> recognized in early stages. Children left out in the
> streets on cold winter mornings are brought into
> the homes of other parents: one takes responsibil-
> ity for morning comforts, another gives hot
> lunches, and others attempt to talk with the par-
> ents. The community provides for its own! Even
> when a child is beaten, parents closest in proximity
> and bound to a code permeating overlapping inter-
> nal neighborhood networks take it upon them-
> selves to have a "neighborly" chat.
> In the "bucket brigade," parents working on
> reading difficulties pinpoint unusual or abusive
> parent-child relationships during the child's story-
> telling time. The way this is handled is that, "We
> all get together and try to decide who to talk with.
> Sometimes it's the parents, and sometimes [if they
> know there might be repercussions on the child]
> we tell the school psychologist. Call the police?
> Bring in outsiders? Never! 'We handle our own!' "

As can be seen from the forgoing excerpts, child abuse cases in this parochial neighborhood would seldom reach the "officially reported" stage. Instead, the neighborhood would draw upon its vast reservoir of shared norms and values and upon its stable set of internal resources to cope with such problems within the neighborhood setting.

An Anomic Neighborhood. In this neighborhood, which

is adjacent to the just-described parochial area, there is a marked absence of social organizations, of patterns of participation, and of a common identification with the local area or the larger society. The following excerpts are taken from field notes on this neighborhood: "Although people talk a long time with us, they do not see or talk to each other. They can't rely on one another for help. The values people have are not that much different from each other. On rare occasions where neighbors are induced to talk together with us, there is amazement that their concerns are mutual." Given that an anomic neighborhood is least likely to influence, mobilize, or alter the values of its residents through any form of resocialization, we should expect individuals in this neighborhood to handle child abuse cases quite differently from the way that individuals in the parochial neighborhood do. The typical response in an anomic neighborhood is the "dependency relationship" model. The following field notes illustrate this:

> Here a child abuse problem is simply dealt with. As the neighbors say: "Call the police—it's not my kid." Or perhaps they call the elementary school principal. No attempt is made by neighbors to address the problem. The closest one comes to this is an actual court case where the family engaging in continued child abuse blamed and "threatened to get" the principal for having their child taken from their home. Here, if there is a problem, "it's either call the police or wait until someone's dead or something."
>
> Also, once child abuse is cited and the family finally gets plugged into the professional treatment system, there is total dependence. A "lock-in" model results wherein the *only* people that the family communicates with are the professionals— and the same neighborhood indifference exists, only to "egg on" the abuser and perhaps provoke further abuse.

Thus, we can see that in the anomic neighborhood, child maltreatment cases, if they are dealt with at all, are referred to resources external to the neighborhood. Reliance on external professional agencies can easily lead to an all-encompassing dependence on the part of clients, especially those who reside in an anomic neighborhood where there are *no* other ties to internal or external resources.

Implications for Practitioners

The neighborhood analysis that I have developed can help child protection agencies begin to see the available community resources and social patterns in their service areas. Using diagnostic tools based on the typology of neighborhoods, agency staff members can determine the proper extent and character of outreach efforts. For example, they can evaluate the need for high-cost, trained professional workes in local subcenters. They can examine the functioning of existing programs of primary prevention and determine what, if any, additional steps need to be taken. In addition to identifying types of neighborhoods, practitioners can set about identifying those persons who comprise the natural problem-solving networks of a given neighborhood. If agencies maintain contact with any of the network members—particularly with the neighborhood activists—the possibility of primary prevention, as well as treatment and followup, of maltreatment cases will be greatly enhanced. Such efforts can be organized through the use of systematic survey research, carried out either directly by the agencies or by local residents who have been trained to gather such knowledge about the networks in their communities. (Chapter Five suggests one way to "map" the problems of child maltreatment in a community as a basis for undertaking intervention at the neighborhood level.)

For professionals interested in preventive intervention, the importance of lay problem-solving networks is paramount. Professional interventions seen in a neighborhood context are synonymous with community development in that they involve increasing the adaptive and problem-solving capacities of the communities through an infusion of resources. Even more importantly, they involve restructuring functional relationships within communities and between communities and outside resources. The consequence of such interventions is to make people in communities better able to deal with ongoing problems and to change through their own efforts, as well as to use professional expertise in a more effective and differentiated way. If neighborhood problem-solving networks do not exist in communities, practitioners can help create them. They can foster grassroots communication by establishing "telephone trees" in which volunteers contact neighborhood families on a regular basis. Practitioners can survey neighborhoods to determine individuals' needs, their common interests, and their special service requirements, such as childcare, medical regimes and appointments, and advice for employment benefits. By grouping needs and establishing ongoing communication among those with shared interests, practitioners can "organize" neighborhoods for service without forcing them to rely heavily on outside resources or constant professional follow-up.

Citizen advisory groups may be established in those neighborhoods where child protection or social service agencies are located. Such efforts may be initiated by the agencies or by neighborhoods that desire additional services. A critical aspect is the number of formal service organizations that use the physical facilities of local schools, parks, and playgrounds or other resources having special purpose designations. By treating the staff and programs of such agencies as "traffic intersection" points, child protective practitioners can maintain effective contact with the neighborhood and also design outreach prevention and treatment programs. Chapters Six, Seven, and Eight offer some guidance for achieving these goals.

CHAPTER 5

Identifying High-Risk Neighborhoods

James Garbarino
Deborah Sherman

In this chapter, we will try to reinforce the view that child maltreatment should be treated as a social problem. It is our belief
that some neighborhoods work *for* parents and children while
others work *against* them. Areas are "low risk" if they help support families, and "high risk" if they work against families.
Low-risk neighborhoods help to overcome a family's internal
weaknesses, while high-risk neighborhoods compound internal
family problems. Thus, a high-risk neighborhood makes child
maltreatment more likely than would be predicted on the basis
of a family's own characteristics, while a low-risk neighborhood
makes child maltreatment less likely.

But can one tell a high-risk from a low-risk area? What
does a high-risk area look like? And what can one do once an
area has been identified as high-risk? The previous chapters discussed ways to classify neighborhoods on the basis of their iden-

94

tity, interaction, and linkages. In this chapter, we will discuss a strategy for "screening" neighborhoods as a basis for identifying high-risk areas. We will present both a complex statistical analysis and a simpler "short form" so that people with a variety of skills and resources can make use of the material. This will set the stage for intervention as described in Chapters Six, Seven, and Eight. First, though, we need to introduce the concept of "ecological mapping," for it is by means of such mapping that we begin to better understand—and better cope with—child maltreatment.

Our Tools

In an excellent article on scientific method, Bronfenbrenner and Mahoney (1975) recount the efforts of Louis DiCarlo and John Gentry, who discovered that naturally occurring radiation is responsible for some birth defects:

> Some years ago, Dr. Louis DiCarlo, then the director of a speech clinic in Syracuse, New York, was surprised by the unexpectedly high proportion of cases of cleft palate coming from certain sparsely populated counties in upstate New York. He was so struck by the phenomenon that he reported it to the district office of the U.S. Public Health Service directed by Dr. John Gentry. Gentry responded by doing what public health physicians have done for decades; he started putting up pins on a map, in this instance a map of New York State, one pin for each case, not only of cleft palate but of all reported congenital malformations (which are deformities present at birth). When all the pins were in place, they made a pattern that Gentry found familiar. Where had he seen it before? After some effort, he remembered. It was in a geology course, on a map of igneous rock formations in New York State. Igneous rocks are those that were originally extracted from within the earth's surface. They are found in mountainous areas and glacial deposits. What is more, some of these rocks emit natural

radiation, and, as Gentry knew, radiation had been suspected as a possible source of cleft palate and other deformities present at birth [p. 2].

Odd though it may seem, this story has much to tell us about identifying neighborhoods that are at risk for child maltreatment, for just as cases of cleft palate can be mapped, and their underlying ecological causes exposed, so can cases of child abuse and neglect.

Thus, Figure 1 maps reported cases of child maltreatment in a metropolitan county. As can be seen, these cases are plotted on a map of the twenty neighborhood areas of a city.

Figure 1. Child Maltreatment Cases for a Metropolitan County
(expressed as cases per 1,000 families)

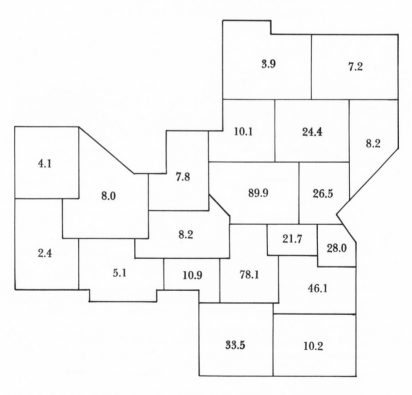

Like Gentry, we will now match this map with another, one that plots some important facts about the local ecology. Based on our understanding of the social conditions that produce child maltreatment, we will use a map that plots both stresses and supports for families. Essentially, this is the approach that we have taken in numerous recent studies (Garbarino, 1976; Garbarino and Crouter, 1978b; Garbarino, Crouter, and Sherman, 1977). But how, specifically, did we draw up this map and what have we found through its use? The technical reports tell the full story, but we can summarize our method and results here as a basis for describing our case study of two particular neighborhoods.

Child Maltreatment Data. State and local child maltreatment reports were used to generate the map of reported child maltreatment (abuse and/or neglect). Rates of maltreatment ranged from 2.4 to 89.9 cases per 1,000 families. Previous work (for example, Banagale and McIntire, 1975; Benjamin and others, 1976; Garbarino and Crouter, 1978a) suggested that reporting in this county has become reliable enough to allow use of the data for statistical analysis. To find out more about the data, we looked at the source of the reports. We wanted to know whether the reports came to child protective services from an institutional source such as a doctor, hospital, or social service worker or from a private citizen—for example, a relative, friend, or neighbor.

When we looked at the reports from this standpoint, we made two interesting findings. First, reports from some areas characteristically came from private citizens, whereas reports from other areas came from institutional representatives. It was in the more affluent areas that reports tended to come from private citizens, while in the less affluent areas reports tended to come from institutional sources. This finding squares with Gil's national survey (1970) in which he found that people from minority groups and people with little formal education were not inclined to report child abuse to the authorities but instead would personally involve themselves in the situation. (Clearly, one can map the source of the reports when screening neighborhoods. This may reveal different needs for public awareness campaigns depending upon the area in which one is working.)

Second, when we analyzed reports from agencies and private citizens separately, we found the same relationships between the rate of maltreatment and economic and social conditions. The two different sources of information were giving the same answers. These results led us to believe that the report data were a good reflection of the actual level of child maltreatment in this metropolitan county.

Data on Social Conditions. Based on previous work (Garbarino, 1976, 1977a; Garbarino and Crouter, 1978a, 1978b), we selected five variables on which to focus in developing our map of social conditions—two to indicate the level of economic resources and three to indicate important social factors.

The two economic variables we chose were (1) percent of households with incomes less than $8,000 a year and (2) percent of households with incomes greater than $15,000 a year. Our hypothesis was that these two measures would provide a good indication of the financial resources of families in the neighborhoods. Other analyses (for example, Garbarino, 1975; National Academy of Sciences, 1976) suggested that the impact of income on families is largely a qualitative matter; that is, income differences affect families by placing them in different economic life-styles. The U.S. Department of Labor prepares model budgets based on this idea. Each budget indicates the income needed to achieve a particular style of living. But we find it useful to go beyond the commonly used category of "poverty" and instead to use the categories of "struggling" and "comfortable." In the former, life is a struggle because its necessities are barely available. In the latter, one can be comfortable with prudent management. Thus, we chose to identify two dividing lines: (1) less than $8,000 per year in 1975 dollars ("struggling") and (2) more than $15,000 per year in 1975 dollars ("comfortable").

These three indicators were chosen as a measurement of the social resources in the neighborhood: (1) percent of female-headed households, (2) percent of married mothers (with children under age eighteen) in the labor force, and (3) percent of less-than-one-year residents. Single-parent families, working mothers of dependent children, and transients all are drains on the neighborhood as a support system for families. People in these categories tend to be concerned with meeting their own pressing needs. When a neighborhood consists mainly of families in these categories, it has few people who are "free from drain" (Collins and Pancoast, 1976). This means that it will also have few of the established people who usually provide the focal point for the "natural helping networks" that are so important to families coping with stress.

Matching the Two Maps. In our statistical comparison of the two maps, we found that the five indicators of social conditions accounted for a great deal (80 percent) of the variation in child maltreatment among the neighborhoods. The economic character of the neighborhood was very important, but the information about family "drain" was important in its own right. When put together, a neighborhood's economic *and* social character provided a very good account of neighborhood differences in child maltreatment. In Figure 2, we show how well our "prediction" of each neighborhood's rate of maltreatment (based on its economic and social character) matches the actual rate.

As can be seen, many areas are quite near to the diagonal line in Figure 2, representing a one-to-one correspondence between actual and predicted rates of child maltreatment. But areas 9 and 5 reveal very large discrepancies (actual cases of child maltreatment minus predicted cases). They have very similar predicted rates (52 cases per 1,000 families for area 9 and 59 cases for area 5), but their actual rates differ markedly (26 cases for area 9 versus 89 cases for area 5). These are the areas most in need of additional explanation; thus, Table 1 compares them in a variety of economic conditions, social characteristics, and attitudes. While the survey data show that these areas are comparable in economic and social terms, these data also reveal that there are less positive attitudes and feelings about life in area 5 than in area 9. This finding suggests that area 5 is a nonsupportive neighborhood environment.

A Tale of Two Neighborhoods

Once the degree of "risk" for a neighborhood has been established through the statistical mapping procedure, more informal interviewing methods can be used to assess specific

Figure 2. Actual and Predicted Rates of Total Child Maltreatment
(per 1,000 families) for Twenty Douglas County, Nebraska,
Subareas (1976 report data)

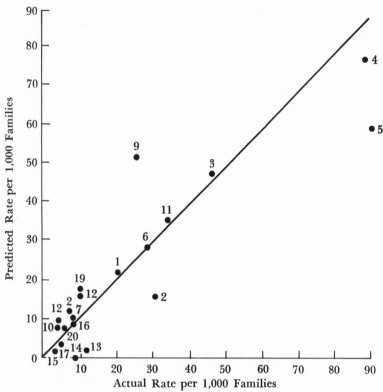

Source: 1976 report data provided by the Douglas County, Nebraska,
Child Protection Services Division, Gene Mallory, director.

needs for services. The findings from our mapping study were
confirmed in an intensive investigation of two neighborhoods,
one low-risk and the other high-risk. In this study, we conducted interviews with a randomly drawn sample of families
from each area as well as with others who were familiar with the
neighborhoods. The two neighborhoods have similar economic
profiles but otherwise are as different as night and day, as the
following remarks from the interviews reveal:

Table 1. Comparison of Two Discrepant Subareas
Designated High and Low Risk for Child Maltreatment

Comparison Variable	Area 9 (Low Risk)	Area 5 (High Risk)
A. Factors in Screening Neighborhoods		
1. Percent of households with incomes less than $8,000	56	60
2. Percent of households with incomes greater than $15,000	7	4
3. Percent of female-headed households	16	21
4. Percent of married mothers (with children under age eighteen) in labor force	39	36
5. Percent of population resident less than one year	52	43
B. Other Factors		
1. Percent of single-family housing	31	11
2. Composite assessment of housing market (1 = growing, 5 = badly deteriorated)	3	4
3. Percent dissatisfied with housing	14	26
4. Percent rating neighborhood conditions as "poor" or "fair"	42	67
5. Percent strongly desiring to move	22	32
6. Percent indicating "good neighbors" are essential neighborhood feature	95	85
7. Percent of persons describing their neighborhood as least desirable area in which to live	2	9

Neighborhood Public Image

Low-risk: "That's one of the most sedate areas" (police officer).
"That's a good quick area" (postman).

High-risk: "That's a little less tranquil. The bars are just pits. The crowd is hoodlums, Hell's Angels, and cowboys" (police officer).
"There's a lot of 'night activity' there" (visiting nurse).

Neighborhood Appearances, Housing, and Public Notices

Low-risk: "The housing, mainly single-family homes, is kept up
            well. Home-improvement activities apparent. Empty
            lots are usually mown, cared for, and look as though
            they are used as play areas" (D. Sherman).

High-risk: "It's low rent there (sixty-five dollars per month).
            They don't have good locks. There are no screens
            on the windows. Cockroaches are all over. We're
            concerned about the children's safety since the
            second-floor windows are without screens" (visiting
            nurse).

            "FOR SALE and APARTMENT FOR RENT signs
            dot the neighborhood. BEWARE OF THE DOG
            signs are also noticeable" (D. Sherman).

Social Characteristics

Low-risk: "This is a solidly middle-income area, and upwardly
            mobile. There is a tendency to change to private
            doctors and to see our organization as for low-
            income groups only" (visiting nurse).

High-risk: "There is a dichotomy in the neighborhood. There
            is a significant number of rather stable, well-put to-
            gether families that live in their own homes. Then
            there is the other group of people (and their chil-
            dren comprise about *half* of the local students) who
            are living in apartments or who rent broken-down
            homes. They kind of move in and out of the neigh-
            borhood. There are a number of families where
            we'll have the kids for three or four months, they
            will leave, and then we'll have them again" (elemen-
            tary school principal).

Neighborhood Change or Stability

Low-risk: "I see it as a stable neighborhood. People have
            roots in the neighborhood. It's not a very mobile
            place" (visiting nurse).

High-risk: "The parents cling to this school as a sign of hope. The neighborhood is facing a lot of change and deterioration. . . . They probably felt threatened by the construction of the interstate through the neighborhood. . . . Just this year we've had several new cases of loiterers, and some families report burglaries where they have never happened before. . . . The parish bought up a building opposite the school which had been recently turned into a rough place" (parochial school principal).

Neighborhood Life-Style and Quality

Fifty-five percent of the families in the high-risk neighborhood think that their neighbors are unfriendly, as compared to 38 percent in the low-risk area.

Low-risk: "We have very few cases there, only six families with children" (visiting nurse).

High-risk: "That's an area that needs plenty of scrutiny as far as quality of life" (director of a neighborhood community center).

"There's stealing from each other" (visiting nurse). "That's one of our heaviest caseloads, both as number of families and as problems within each family. Alcoholism is quite a big problem. . . . There are mental health problems, a very high death rate, a high birthrate to unmarried mothers, poor nutrition. . . . Medical knowledge is only of emergency care. . . . Many of the girls are early school dropouts" (visiting nurse).

Child Abuse and Neglect

In the low-risk neighborhood, 86 percent of the families have parents present when children return home from school versus only 25 percent in the high-risk neighborhood. In the high-risk neighborhood, 13 percent of the families have no one home when children return from school versus 0 percent in the low-risk neighborhood. In the high-risk neighborhood, 9 percent of the families leave children alone when they are home sick from school versus 0 percent in the low-risk neighborhood.

Low-risk: "There used to be a number of cases there, but now it will be real hard to find one" (child protective services worker).

"I would say that child abuse and neglect [are] not as much a problem in the area as in others. Most of the referrals are for neglect—about 80 percent" (visiting nurse).

High-risk: "There are probably a significant number of five-to-eight-year-olds at school who got themselves up this morning. They may or may not have been at their own homes, but they got themselves to school and took care of their needs" (elementary school principal).

"There were probably about six to eight suspected cases of physical abuse last year. We see neglect cases maybe twenty-five to thirty times a year at [X] school, and as high as fifty times in [Y] school" (elementary school principal).

Neighborhood Involvement of Families

In the high-risk neighborhood, 32 percent of the families are reluctant about exchanging any form of help with neighbors versus 8 percent in the low-risk neighborhood.

Low-risk: "[Z] school has an active, ongoing Girl Scout troop" (Girl Scout leader).

High-risk: "[X] and [Y] schools are just beginning to be organized by our fieldworkers" (Girl Scout leader).

"About 35 percent of the parents are active with the school. On a scale from +3 to −3, I'd rate the level of activism as 0" (parochial school principal).

"We have the least amount of input from them compared to other centers . . . we're not as close to that neighborhood. Nobody is" (director of a community center).

Social Relations-Informal Supports

Only 4 percent of the low-risk neighborhood's families say it was difficult to adjust to living there versus 18 percent in the high-risk neighborhood.

Low-risk: "These women often rely on the help available to them through their families. One client of mine lives next door to her mother-in-law to whom she turns for help" (visiting nurse).

High-risk: "The family unit is not real strong here" (parochial school principal).

"The women sometimes form a 'buddy system,' but there is not a lot of interlinking between them. . . . They don't know very many people. They don't associate very much. They don't have a lot of family supports. They may be on bad terms with the family. This area is sometimes a hide-out place for them. . . . There are a lot of teenage girls with their babies who want to get away from their families downtown" (visiting nurse).

"People don't trust each other much. . . . There is stealing among some of the neighbors, while there is some help among the mothers" (visiting nurse).

Using the Information

Our research leads us to believe that the quality of a neighborhood depends on both its material and social resources. As Donald Warren showed in Chapter Four, some neighborhoods are economically rich and socially poor, while others are socially rich and economically poor. Although in practice we usually are most concerned with economically poor neighborhoods, we also need to know which areas are socially well off and which are socially impoverished when we devise helping strategies and allocate scarce resources. If a neighborhood "works" well, we don't want to barge in and disrupt it. As Kromkowski (1976) noted: "The organic life of a neighborhood, created by the persons who live in a particular geographic area, is always a fragile reality. A neighborhood's character is determined by a host of factors, but most significantly by the kinds of relationships that neighbors have with each other. A neighborhood is not a sovereign power—it can rarely write its own agenda. Although neighborhoods differ in a host of ways, a healthy neighborhood has pride in the neighborhood, care of homes, security for children, and respect for each other" (p. 228).

However, in cases where the actual rate of child maltreatment is substantially greater than the predicted rate (as in area 5 in Figure 2), hypotheses can be generated. For example, one might "blame" the high rate of abuse and neglect on stressful circumstances peculiar to that area. Or one might consider the possibility that demographic trends have produced a situation in which there are not enough mature families to exert a stabilizing influence on the neighborhood. The value of the screening process is that it tells one where to look and offers some suggestions about what to look for. Note that among the neighborhoods accurately predicted by our screening are areas that have both low and high actual rates of maltreatment. Thus, even though the difference between actual and predicted rate of maltreatment for a neighborhood is small, the area may still need help. Such neighborhoods simply conform better than neighborhoods that are not "well predicted" to what can be expected on the basis of economic and social characteristics. We can, in fact, see our task in this book as one of devising ways to decrease risk by making all neighborhoods have fewer cases of maltreatment than would be predicted. That would represent solid progress and would mean that we were being effective as social engineers.

In addition to knowing whether the actual rate of maltreatment is high or low, we need to know whether we are dealing with a high- or low-risk neighborhood. Once a "diagnosis" has been made and confirmed, it can provide the basis for further case studies and ultimately for intervention. Such intervention may include efforts to stimulate natural helping networks and better communication between professionals and residents. As a result of the screening procedure, child protective services can better exercise both diagnostic and advocacy roles with

respect to families and children. Moreover, limited agency resources can be better allocated, the professional can be integrated into existing support systems as a source of feedback,
and neighborhood groups can be advised of likely targets for
community action.

A Short Form for Screening Neighborhoods

Unfortunately, many agencies will not have the resources
or expertise necessary to use the statistical techniques employed
in our screening procedure. If there is no college or university
nearby, it may be difficult to find an expert consultant. And if
an agency does not have access to a government research and
planning office, the fieldworkers will usually be left to their
own devices. With this in mind, we offer a simplified version of
the screening approach, one that does not require the use of
complex statistics or computerized analysis.

1. Select appropriate geographic units. These will vary somewhat from place to place depending upon local history and
   record-keeping policies.
2. Obtain the necessary data. These include both the reported
   rate of child maltreatment cases (by family) per 1,000 families (or per 100 families if the units are very small) and the
   percent of families in each area below some income level
   that means "struggling." This would be approximately
   $10,500 in 1979 dollars.
3. Plot the relationship of low income to child maltreatment.
   For our data it looks like this:

Child Maltreatment Rate (per 1,000 families)	Percent of Families with Income Less than $8,000
89.9	64.0
78.1	65.5
46.1	74.0
33.5	51.3
28.0	56.0
26.5	50.1
24.4	44.3

Child Maltreatment Rate (per 1,000 families)	Percent of Families with Income Less Than $8,000
21.7	31.8
10.9	20.0
10.2	16.3
10.1	30.0
8.2	34.3
8.2	15.0
8.0	5.0
7.8	5.8
7.2	19.4
5.1	8.4
4.1	8.1
3.9	22.2
2.4	13.2

4. Look for discrepant neighborhoods. In general, the more a neighborhood is characterized by low-income families, the more child maltreatment it will have. But look for cases that depart from this pattern.

5. Develop hypotheses about discrepant neighborhoods. Ask yourself: Why do these discrepancies exist? In developing hypotheses to guide further information gathering and ultimate intervention, use both numerical data (for example, information on single-parent households and transience) and informal interviews with people who know the neighborhoods and what makes them tick.

Once you have done the background work to assess the level of neighborhood risk, you have set the stage for action. In Chapters Six and Seven, Diane Pancoast and Alice Collins provide a strategy, as well as some guidelines, for proceeding.

CHAPTER 6

Finding and Enlisting Neighbors to Support Families

Diane L. Pancoast

Supportive social relationships are important to families who must cope with the stresses of being parents. When such relationships are weak or absent, families are less able to cope with these stresses, and child maltreatment is more likely to occur. Supportive social relationships generally form relatively enduring patterns or "natural helping networks." In this and the following chapter, Allice Collins and I argue that professionals can help to strengthen these networks and thereby prevent child maltreatment. Our approach, which we call "the neighborhood consulting model," grew out of our experiences as social workers concerned with community-based preventive services.

When our collaboration first began, Collins was involved in a research and demonstration project with family daycare, and I was working in a project providing services to discharged patients with chronic mental illnesses. Although our experiences had been very different on the surface, we soon realized that there were underlying similarities. We both were interested in going beyond formally organized services in order to identify and strengthen informal caretaking mechanisms. Working in different neighborhoods and with different populations, we both had discovered individuals in these communities who were actively involved with the groups that we regarded as our target populations. Collins and her colleagues had found that family daycare involved a web of relationships of givers and users in which some daycare givers played key roles as consultants, referral agents, and general supporters of the daycare system. In another project, with chronic mental patients, I had identified the boarding home operators as important, if ignored, figures in the community "system" of aftercare for discharged patients. In the years that followed, we continued to gain experience with such networks in our practice and to learn about others from both published reports and the experiences of our students at the School of Social Work, Portland State University, and we eventually wrote a book about these networks (Collins and Pancoast, 1976). As the evidence has accumulated, we have become convinced that our model is workable in a number of settings and for many problems that call for blends of prevention and treatment. Before turning specifically to families at risk for maltreatment, however, I will describe the common properties of natural helping networks as a review and expansion of what has been said by the authors of earlier chapters.

Natural Helping Networks as Support Systems

We are all involved in relationships that include the exchange of various kinds of help. This help can take the form of tangible resources and activities as well as of emotional support and feedback (Caplan, 1974). Sometimes help comes from strangers or slight acquaintances, but more frequently it comes from friends, relatives, and coworkers. We usually feel that we are providers as well as recipients of assistance, and we keep rough accounts of our "social security" and social indebtedness. Viewed in the aggregate, these ties among individuals form networks that indirectly link a given participant to many others through intermediaries. Often these networks contain individuals who are especially well-connected, whose relationships with other members of the network are numerous and rich. We have called these people "central figures" or "natural helpers." These individuals often link together people who were previously unknown to each other. They are "matchmakers." Sometimes their central position in the network results from their personal attributes, sometimes from the special character of a situation. Most often it involves both.

By thinking about helping networks as social supports, we can focus our attention on the specific members of a network and the character of their relationships. This information can be useful to professionals in assessing the social strengths of a particular family at risk for child abuse or neglect. It may reveal possibilities for creating links that will increase the resources available to the family. Another approach to networks is to understand them as collectivities. This leads us to identify their central figures and to try to strengthen the role of these natural helpers through consultation. In this way, professionals may help families who are linked to the central figures without ever having direct contact with those families.

Central figures may not exist in every network, and there are families who are not involved in any network. But networks and central figures have been found in such a variety of social settings that an approach based on identifying them and offering services to and through them seems worth trying. This is a good investment because, once the central figures have been identified, the professional has an opportunity to affect a large number of families with a minimum of effort and without destroying the positive coping abilities of the families or increasing their dependence on formal services.

Consultation to Central Figures

In order to be successful, an intervention program with central figures must be oriented to prevention and have broad goals. Even though consultation programs affect many families relative to the expenditure of professional time, they seldom

can be precisely targeted to families involved in abuse or neglect. However, since the "targets" in our approach are networks, not families, high-risk networks can be given special
attention.

Severe abuse occurs relatively infrequently in any population; instances of inadequate parenting and of neglect are much
more common. We believe that many of these milder forms of
maltreatment may be quite amenable to constructive intervention by central figures and the members of their networks. Ad-
mittedly, there may be obstacles. Those who must deal directly
with severe abuse cases may feel overwhelmed by the demands
of their case loads. Often they do not feel that they have the
"luxury" of planning a program for families who are experiencing only moderate difficulty. Even overburdened agencies, however, may be able to free the time of one worker to explore
preventive approaches in a limited, pilot demonstration project.
If services are organized on a geographical basis, caseworkers in
a particular unit might also be able to pool their knowledge
about local resources and central figures. One such agency in
Portland, Oregon, was able to free a worker on a part-time basis
to consult with two central figures who were managers of run-
down trailer courts where the incidence of neglect and abuse
was particularly high (Watson, 1970).

Agencies in the community concerned with broad aspects
of family life may be more likely sponsors of a program of consultation to central figures than are child protective agencies
themselves. Health care organizations that employ visiting
nurses or outreach workers, child guidance clinics, neighborhood-based service centers, daycare services, and organizations
that deal with special disabilities such as mental retardation are
all possible sponsors. In some cases, there may be strong enough
ties among the families who use these services that central figures who are not geographically linked can be identified. For
instance, a social worker developing services for mentally retarded children in a large, sparsely populated county in a western state found that one parent of a retarded child was serving
as a natural helper. The worker reported: "In discussion with
[other professionals], the name of Mrs. Morris was heard many

times. As I began calling on the families of mentally retarded children to talk about their situations, offer them information, and so forth, I often heard the Morris name mentioned. Some others had talked to Mrs. Morris about finding schooling; others had talked to her after learning about their own child's retardation; several knew Mrs. Morris through the Association for Retarded Children" (Collins, Pancoast, and Dunn, 1977, p. 38).

One advantage of having a broadly focused agency sponsor a program of consultation to central figures is that the negative consequences of associating the program with the problem of child abuse can be avoided. In Chapter Eight, David Olds discusses this issue as it affects a program directly aimed at high-risk families. In that program, it was felt that labeling and stigmatizing such families as potentially abusive would discourage their participation. In offering consultation to central figures, the danger is not one of discouraging participation, since no one is being asked to participate in a formal program; rather, it is one of introducing concepts and concerns that may be alien to the network and may have negative effects upon it. The purpose of providing consultation to the central figure is not to create a spy or sleuth who will ferret out cases of abuse and report them to the authorities. Instead, it is to learn how the central figure is already helping families and to offer some advice and support to strengthen his or her role. Sponsorship by an agency with broad purposes helps to keep the purpose of the consultation clear.

Whatever the sponsorship of the program, however, care must be taken to explain its purposes to other workers in the agency, to other agencies in the community, to funding sources, and to governing boards. It may not be easy to explain the expected outcomes clearly at the beginning, since much depends on the kinds of central figures that are found. But the broad intent can be described and plans made to provide ongoing progress reports as the program develops. Professional cooperation provides a supportive community climate for neighborhood consultation. I will return to this question when I present an approach to identifying central figures. For now, I will assume that an agency has been found that is willing to try an experimental program. On that premise, I will discuss the characteristics of central figures and their relevance to programs aimed at improving family life.

What Central Figures Are Like

Individuals are linked to one another in various ways, and the size and character of networks can differ from one type of relationship to another. Kinship is one basis for relationships, power is another. Here, however, we are concerned with supportive relationships. The quality of mutual support, or helping, is what defines the networks that interest us. In order to work with these networks, we may have to concern ourselves with other kinds of linkages, such as those that derive from kinship or a common work setting, but our main focus is on supportive networks. None of us sees *all* kin as actual or potential supportive resources, nor do we develop such relationships with all those with whom we work.

How Does One Become a Central Figure? Central figures in networks that are mutually supportive attain their centrality by playing key helping roles and by matching resources to need. Calling these people "central figures" highlights their role within the network itself. Calling them "natural helpers" emphasizes the personal attributes they bring to relationships in their networks. Since both aspects usually are important, both terms will be used.

The central position of persons in their networks may result from their stability. The staff member who "outlives" a succession of other workers may become important to the organization simply by virtue of the greater experience he or she possesses. Similarly, someone who lives in an area longer than anyone else may become an important resource for newcomers. This stability is relative to that of others in the network, of course. In such highly unstable situations as migrant labor camps, trailer courts, or hangouts that attract runaway teenagers, central figures may be only slightly more stable than any of the other participants and almost indistinguishable to an outside observer.

Occupying a "crossroads" position can also contribute to

the central position of an individual in a network. This may be geographical, as in the case of a person who works in an area adjacent to a gathering place or whose house or apartment is centrally located. The position may simply involve visibility, as in the case of an individual who works in a grocery store or drugstore where he or she interacts with many people everyday. Even a person who merely takes daily walks around the neighborhood will see many more neighbors than one who spends the day inside. Of course, not all people who are located in a busy place or who make themselves visible are central figures, but it is unlikely that a more or less isolated person will become a central figure. The telephone is a tremendous asset to people who want to stay in contact with others, but such contacts are usually not sustained for any length of time without periodic face-to-face interaction.

Some people are central because they have access to valuable resources. The person with access to jobs, social services, or governmental agencies may be used by network members for information about these services or as a mediator. In situations of deprivation, one member of the network may have food, clothing, or shelter that he or she can share with others (Stack, 1974). Information about other members of the network or about issues of concern to the network is another resource that the central figure may possess. The information can come from prior personal experience as well as from outside sources. Mothers of very young children may find especially useful the advice of another mother whose children are slightly older. Parents who learn that their child has a disability or serious illness may seek out other parents who have coped with the same problem. Once again, experience per se will not produce "centrality," for some people may be unwilling or unable to share their experience with others. But other people are extraordinarily good at empathizing with fellow sufferers. This has been shown in programs that link widows with the recently bereaved, in programs that link women who have had mastectomies with mastectomy patients, and in other self-help programs (Caplan and Killilea, 1976).

"Freedom from Drain." Personal attributes are also im-

portant for converting opportunities to become central figures in networks into actual positions of centrality. Natural helpers are people who possess a lively interest in others. They are good listeners and have genuine empathy with the people in their networks. They are able to give advice and support without antagonizing the recipient. They do not make others feel indebted to them. Rather, they see their activities as what anyone would do in a similar situation, as nothing out of the ordinary, and as part of a mutual exchange and sharing. Although their circumstances are similar to those of others in their networks, they exhibit what has been called "freedom from drain" (Collins and Pancoast, 1976), and they can handle stresses that overwhelm others. In addition to their situational availability, natural helpers are emotionally accessible. They are never too busy to listen, they can draw others out, and they are willing to reach out to strangers and to recontact others "just to see how they are doing" or to learn the result of a particular piece of advice.

If we think about natural helpers that we have known, we can probably recognize many of these qualities. We also know, however, that these helpers are real people and therefore not paragons of virtue or flawless experts in interpersonal relationships. Natural helpers develop networks of people with whom they feel comfortable. They may not be particularly effective with people outside the network. Their behavior reflects their own values and is influenced by the culture they share with other members of the network. Their values may not be congruent with those of a professional caregiver. It is important, especially in such a sensitive area as childrearing, to initially evaluate the practices of the natural helper in terms of the network, not according to other standards. Similarly, the natural helper may sometimes violate professional standards of confidentiality, although most central figures are very selective about divulging information, giving advice, and sharing personal experiences. Again, the professional must be careful to evaluate the natural helper, not in terms of professional standards of conduct appropriate for a formally organized helping service, but in terms of effective performance as a helper in the network. All these considerations involve special difficulties when we are dealing with child maltreatment; given the alternative of inaction, however, they are well worth addressing.

The professional always needs to keep in mind that central figures owe their position in the network to the confidence that network members place in them. The professional cannot create a central figure and may jeopardize the usefulness of an existing one if anything is done to undermine the central figure's position in the network. We think that consultation is a promising way of strengthening the role of the central figure without changing the basic relationships and understandings of the network. Obviously, any intervention by an outside professional must be skillfully done and undertaken only when the network is well understood.

Networks, Central Figures, and Families Involved in Child Maltreatment

Turning now to the kinds of networks that are relevant to families who are at risk for child maltreatment, I will discuss some of the factors that contribute to this problem and what natural helpers might be able to do, or are already doing, to help families-in-need.

Sick Parents. A small group of psychotic parents accounts for some of the most lurid instances of child abuse. Often, when such cases finally come to light, persons emerge who have been deeply concerned about these families but have felt helpless to intervene directly with the family. Sometimes, however, one of these persons had become upset enough to make a report to an official agency. Other abusing families come to the attention of the child protective agency through police or hospital staff. In these extreme cases, the pressing need is not for support and resources for the family but for detection of the problem so that the child can be removed from a dangerous situation. Even though emotionally disturbed parents usually interact very little with their neighbors, there are often people in the neighborhood who are aware that the family is behaving strangely. Grocery checkers, milkmen, pharmacists, and others who provide commercial services may also become aware of such behavior.

Since the goal here is to increase the reporting of cases, agencies concerned with protecting children might consider extending their efforts to educate potential reporters of child abuse. Such educational efforts should focus on the specific nature of reporting laws and the need of children for protection. The agency should also examine its own procedures to see that people who report cases of child abuse are treated well and kept informed of what the agency is doing about the cases. Once direct agency contact with natural helpers is initiated, the consultant may be able to assist a natural helper in reporting a family to the child protective agency.

Difficult Children. Some children present severe problems for parents because of physical or emotional disabilities. The parents of a difficult child may need information about the child's condition and how to care for him or her, occasional relief from the constant pressures of caretaking, and a great deal of supportive understanding of the problems with which they are coping. Friends, neighbors, and relatives are all potential sources of assistance. A professional worker concerned about such a family may be able to locate natural helpers in the family's existing network or to encourage a natural helper to reach out to the family. Natural helpers among the parents who are using special services for their children are also a potential source of support. Families can exchange services such as babysitting. Families that are coping with the problems of caring for a disabled child can provide information and role models for families that are not handling their children as successfully. Such interaction might be promoted by an organized parent group, but a professional who is working with a population of "special" children could also perform this matchmaking function by introducing a successful family to a less successful one and then allowing further contacts to develop spontaneously.

Inappropriate Attitudes and Expectations About Child-rearing. Parents who value severe punishment and who have highly unrealistic expectations about the normal course of child development may become abusive when their children fail to meet these expectations. Parents may neglect their children by rejecting them, by not understanding them, and by not supplying the basic necessities for healthy growth and development. A family that is involved in a healthy network of relationships is unlikely to develop such patterns because the members of the network can provide different perspectives on the needs of the children and on ways to meet these needs; when a child is rejected by its parents, others in the network may be able to offer compensatory care. In general, then, inappropriate attitudes and expectations are more likely to develop in isolated than in integrated families. There are cases, however, in which families have surrounded themselves with a network of friends who share a world of abnormal rearing. Some observers (for example, Justice and Justice, 1976) suggest that abusive parents are particularly prone to find people like themselves. A young, single mother, for example, may have friends who encourage her to neglect her child. It is in situations like this that a central figure might be especially useful. Such a helper, possibly a babysitter or accessible neighbor, can offer advice and assistance from a position outside the mother's immediate circle but without the authoritative overtones of professional intervention.

It has often been noted that parents of maltreated children are likely to have been maltreated themselves as children. Here again, the family's network, if it consists of relatives, may reinforce negative childrearing patterns. Contact with other families, arranged by a central figure, might present such a family with alternative models of parenting. This subtle form of parent education might produce more lasting changes than would more organized programs. Central figures have other advantages as parent educators. They are often more comfortable with being directive than are professionals. Since the family is free to disregard the central figure's advice, the family may be able to hear and follow it more easily. The central figure may also be more sensitive than a professional to the family's values and thus can couch advice in acceptable terms.

Some central figures also act as surrogate parents for the parents themselves. A parent who had an abusive or neglectful relationship with his or her own parent may find that a relationship with a natural helper provides the good parenting that was lacking earlier in life. The subtle psychological dynamics of such a relationship need not be understood by either party for it to work. Central figures may even use these relationships to compensate for inadequacies in their own upbringing. Some natural helpers, though by no means all of them, may have developed the personal characteristics that have led them to become natural helpers out of their own experiences of deprivation. Again, it is not important that the central figure understand this dynamic if the current relationship benefits both parties.

Stress. When a family's resources are not adequate to cope with its stresses, the resulting frustration, anger, and depression can lead to child abuse or neglect. One way of preventing such an outcome is to reduce the stresses on families. Interventions at this level, while extremely important, are often beyond the capacities of a natural helping network. For example, a network may be able to provide emergency material assistance to tide a family over a crisis such as a temporary job loss or a natural disaster, but fundamental economic improvement for the family usually will be beyond the resources of the network. Moreover, the network itself can sometimes be one of the sources of stress on the family. As already noted, not all networks are benign. Also, families are expected to participate mutually in their networks, and the needs of another member may at times constitute an added burden on a family already experiencing stress. In such instances, a professional working with the family may want to change the network to make it less stressful for the client family. Failing in that, the professional may even try to shift the client to a new network. The other way of preventing stress from overwhelming a family is by increasing the family's resources—well-connected, strong families can handle more stress than isolated, weak ones. The family's access to natural helpers may be a crucial resource. Through professional consultation, central figures can be made aware of the negative consequences of stress. They can be made more sensitive to the difficulties being experienced by families they already know. In some cases, they may also be able to reach out to families on the peripheries of their networks.

Isolation. Isolated families lack the feedback and support provided by involvement in social networks. Children in these families have no allies to whom they can turn if they are being mistreated. The factors that contribute to the family's isolation —geographical distance, unsociable behavior, divergent values or life-style, and so forth—may make it difficult for natural helpers to reach out to them. The children in such families are often more accessible than are the parents, and natural helpers who have contact with the children or who themselves are children may have the most success in establishing contact (see Garbarino and Jacobson, 1978, for a discussion of peer helping among youth). People such as grocery checkers and pharmacists who have contact with the family through commercial transactions and are at the same time sensitive and responsive to other family needs may also be able to reach out to an isolated family.

Before one begins the process of finding natural helping networks, some cautionary notes are in order. A professional who wants to use natural helping networks to reduce the incidence of child maltreatment must always be sensitive to the impact of his or her intervention on the network itself. The professional must understand how the natural helper is functioning in the network before suggesting any changes. This applies to interactions with both current members and new ones. Although the professional must proceed with caution, social networks can nevertheless be helpful to many families, and consultation offered to natural helpers, if sensitively done, can improve their effectiveness.

This chapter and the next deal primarily with an approach to service aimed directly at central figures. By using this approach, families at risk can be aided without direct contact by an agency and before their actions have resulted in severe harm to children. Before we consider this approach, however, we should note that other activities to strengthen helping networks might also be undertaken by concerned agencies. Some of these interventions could be undertaken by an agency or task force specifically concerned with child maltreatment. Others might more appropriately originate elsewhere but could be actively supported by agencies concerned with child abuse and neglect.

Agencies can use a community's information channels (for example, radio, newspaper, and television) to disseminate information about factors that place families in jeopardy. This information can highlight the importance of providing support for families at risk and emphasize the important functions of natural support systems. Natural helpers are often an audience for such media and thus can be expected to use this information. Information about procedures for reporting abuse and neglect also can be given to the media and to community groups. Such procedures should be accessible and simple to use, and the role that the reporting person will play in the case should be explained.

Other activities can be aimed at strengthening existing social support networks. Since central figures tend to operate most successfully when their networks are fairly stable, any action that increases the stability of neighborhoods will benefit helping networks. Child protective agencies should therefore foster neighborhood development projects and other forms of community action. Strengthening neighborhood institutions will also benefit families. Schools, neighborhood centers and associations, churches, recreational establishments, and parks all can contribute to opportunities for social interaction and the communication of information. The better these local facilities are functioning, the more likely it is that families experiencing severe stress or isolation will be detected and offered informal help.

How Can Helping Networks and Central Figures Be Identified?

The first step is to identify natural helpers who are also central figures in helping networks. This is a complex process that must be tailored to the specific situation. Some preliminary work "in the office" can save time during the fieldwork phase, help to focus the goals of the effort more clearly, and produce increased understanding of the project by other professionals and groups.

Consulting with Caseworkers. The records of protective services may hold some information about natural helpers, while the recollections of caseworkers may be even more useful. In either case, the key to success lies in knowing what to look or ask for. Agencies may already have data on rates of reported maltreatment for neighborhoods or census tracts. The technique outlined in Chapter Five may be used with these data to provide a social map of maltreatment in the community. Even if there are no hard data available, workers may have general impressions of where most of the cases originate, and such overviews may give an idea of the range of problems and the differences among neighborhoods.

Specific case records may indicate the names of people making reports. Also, workers may know of individuals who have made reports or have taken an ongoing interest in the affected families. Agencies and their workers sometimes view such people with suspicion, question their motives, and see them as interfering busybodies if they continue to be involved with the family after making a report. Hence, the consultant must make an independent evaluation of the potential usefulness of such people. Some local institutions, such as schools or hospitals, may have been particularly frequent reporters. The consultant will want to know more about the area served by these institutions. When fieldwork begins, the consultant should track down the individual sources of referral. There may be a nurse, doctor, principal, school social worker, or school secretary who is very knowledgeable about the area and particularly sensitive to potential maltreatment cases. This person may also be an important helping figure in the area or know of others who are. He or she may have made a referral after working with a natural helper who was closer to the situation but reluctant to make a report. Successfully rehabilitated families may also be a good source of potential central figures. If the records do not reveal such natural helpers, caseworkers can be interviewed about "what made the difference" for this or that family, with particular attention paid to the mention of natural helpers in the family's social environment.

Finding Central Figures Through Community Referral. Most of this discussion is focused on neighborhoods, since they are probably the most accessible and relevant areas for work with families. Many families, however, do not have significant ties based on locality. Their networks may be based on kinship, on participation in a recreational or religious group, or on friendships originating at their place of work. Other families may move around a good deal. All these factors make it difficult to understand their networks and identify central figures. Still, these families must live *somewhere,* even if it is only for a short time. The children will play with other children in the area and attend the local school. The family will be observed by neighbors, even if no real interaction occurs. Central figures in the neighborhood and in the local institutions will often be aware of these families and can be encouraged to reach out to them. Thus, a neighborhood-based approach may be relevant even when at first it seems impractical.

Other approaches can be used as well. A daycare center may draw from a wide geographic area. Among the families served by the center may be a natural helper. One of the childcare workers in the center may also fill this role. A group of parents with children who have special problems such as developmental disabilities, whether the group is formally organized for mutual support and advocacy or loosely connected by common participation in a service program, is another source of natural helpers. One might think that working parents or parents of handicapped children would be so overwhelmed by their own problems that they would have little time for anyone else's, but experience shows that this is not always the case. Parents become aware of others in the same situation who seem to be coping more successfully than they are, and they turn to them for advice and support. The consultant can ask workers in programs for handicapped children about natural helpers among the staff or parents. Foster parents may be a source of information about natural helpers. Workers who do foster home placements can be queried about foster parents who are particularly involved with neighbors or local groups. Lay persons who are involved in groups that are especially interested in children are another source of information. Agency board members, members of advocacy or lobbying groups, and long-time community leaders are also possible resources.

When the consultant contacts the kinds of people mentioned above, it will be necessary to explain, if only briefly, the reason for seeking information from them. While it is important not to oversell the natural helping program or present it as an alternative to existing services, this contact can provide an opportunity to educate neighborhood advisers about the need for a preventive approach to child maltreatment and the importance of social supports for families. Once sensitized to these concerns, advisers may become aware of natural helping networks that they had not noticed before. The consultant can contact some of these sources more than once to take advantage of new insights and information.

Choosing a Neighborhood. After conferring with the advisers closest at hand and studying all the available data, the consultant should begin to form an impression of how to proceed. In some cases the consultant may see only roadblocks and dead ends. If the results have been disappointing, one of several conditions may be the cause. In the first place, the approach may simply not be feasible in a given area. The incidence of child maltreatment may be so rare and its pattern so random and widely scattered that no appropriate basis for intervention presents itself. Although unlikely, this is a possibility. However, when it is remembered that the focus is on prevention, a considerably larger population is included in the target group, and it is less likely that the approach will seem irrelevant.

Second, the best target for intervention may be outside the range of the agency that is sponsoring the consultant. This situation may result from definitions of the agency's function, its organizational rigidities, its geographic location, or its reputation in the community. Any of these problems might force the consultant to abandon the approach or to look for different auspices under which to work. Even if the project is aborted at this stage, however, the consultant will have gained a useful overview of the problem of child maltreatment as it is seen and handled by important people in the community on a day-to-day basis. In addition, those who have been contacted will gain some fresh perspectives that may in the future prove useful to them in unforeseen ways. Having become more conscious of the importance of social supports for families, for instance, protec-

tive service workers may make more systematic assessments of
the social supports of client families and plan interventions at
this level. Lay people may become more willing to reach out to
vulnerable families.

A third factor that might account for a disappointing response is the consultant's failure to adequately explain to
informants just what kind of information is wanted. If this
problem is suspected, the consultant may want to reevaluate his
or her approach by discussing it with a supervisor or some other
outside expert. Furthermore, most of us are not used to thinking of ourselves or others as natural helpers. There are even
some cultural prohibitions against doing so. As James Garbarino
and S. Holly Stocking noted in Chapter One, people may be
reluctant to identify themselves as helpers because they fear
they will be thought of as interfering meddlers. They may not
name others because they fear this may "expose" that person to
exploitation. This combination of misunderstanding and of
reluctance to divulge information about possible natural helpers
may cause some informants to draw a blank. Again, an explanation of the important role of natural helpers in supporting families is sometimes seen as a criticism of existing services and may
elicit only defensive accounts of what an agency or individual is
doing about child maltreatment or other problems. A reassess-
ment of one's approach should help to spot and correct failures
in communication. And, even though it is difficult to explain
the concept of central figures, the consultant may be encouraged by remembering that the project eventually will have to be
explained to the natural helpers themselves and that explaining
it to professionals will provide opportunities to practice alternative approaches. (Interestingly, sometimes it is harder to make
professionals understand what is wanted than it is to communicate the project's goals to natural helpers.)

Now that the information-gathering phase is complete,
the next step is to pause and take stock. At this stage, the consultant will probably have too much information rather than
too little. A review of this information with a supervisor will be
very helpful in deciding what to do next. It also will help to
keep the agency informed about what the consultant is doing.

Goal Setting. The consultant probably will feel pressured

to select an ambitious goal—either to intervene in the most serious situations or to select a large population at risk. This is a seductive danger. Actually, the first goals should be quite modest. If the largest number of referrals come from an area that is highly disorganized and/or extremely resistant to outsiders, the consultant would do well to gain some experience in a less hostile environment before tackling such problems. Not only will the consultant's skills and confidence be up to the challenge by then, but the agency will be more willing to sponsor a riskier attempt once it has been convinced of the utility of the approach in another setting. A good target for a first effort would be a neighborhood that has a substantial number of maltreatment referrals but also shows some signs of strength, such as residential stability and functioning local institutions and associations, and provides some clues for finding natural helpers. It would be better to select a single neighborhood at first so that fieldwork can be conducted efficiently. Even if the consultant has decided to focus on networks that are not geographically based, the same guidelines for selection should prevail. An organization that is functioning well, has some parental involvement, and serves a population where the risk factors for maltreatment are definitely present but not overwhelming would be a good one to select as the first place to identify natural helpers.

The consultant will be understandably anxious about launching what has been called "the treasure hunt" for natural helpers; this is understandable. Some deadlines for completing fieldwork and regular sessions for reporting to the agency will provide some reassuring structure to what is essentially an unstructured enterprise. The time allotted for locating natural helpers should be generous. In addition to the time already spent in gaining agency approval and background information, which may have been several months, the consultant will probably need to spend three or four months in the field. But this need not be a full-time effort. Interviews and meetings can be worked into other professional and private commitments. The consultant can therefore continue to discharge other duties and to gather additional background information while becoming a visible and trusted person in the neighborhood.

The search for natural helpers resembles an anthropological field trip rather than a social survey or a service program. The purpose of the search is neither to identify social problems and make generalizations, as a survey might do, nor to explain the functions of existing services. The consultant wants to understand how families live in the target area. Where do they work, play, and go to school? What are the unwritten rules governing interaction? What are the networks of interaction? How does information travel? Do families see themselves as transients or have they put down roots?

Central figures can be identified in two ways. A consultant can get information about large networks and identify members of these networks who are particularly rich in connections to other members. Or the same consultant can find "experts" on the target neighborhood and ask them who the leaders and helpers are. Smith (1977) has usefully described these as "breadth-first" and "depth-first" approaches. *If* experts can be identified and interviewed and their information is reliable, the second method is less time consuming than the first. Unless the consultant has a fairly good understanding of the total neighborhood context, however, the only way an expert's information can be validated is by contacting the people who have been nominated and then observing them for a period of time. This may be a time-consuming activity itself. Moreover, once begun, a relationship with a potential central figure may be very difficult to terminate if the consultant decides that the person is not really a natural helper or is a negative influence on the network.

For these reasons, it is wise to proceed simultaneously on all fronts, contacting local leaders and institutions, interviewing possible central figures, observing neighborhood activity patterns, and attending local meetings. Throughout this process, the consultant should keep a low profile, giving enough explanation of the reasons for his or her presence to satisfy the situation's demands, but mostly observing and asking questions. There is no need to worry excessively about "full disclosure" of the project and its goals. Greater clarification of purposes will occur over time as the consultant encounters local residents in a variety of settings. Rather than explicitly stating an interest in preventing child maltreatment or detecting unreported cases, the consultant might say that his or her goal is to understand how families in the neighborhood live and cope with problems, with the intention of supporting them in whatever ways they might find useful.

A good approach during an interview would be to say, "I am interested in this neighborhood, particularly in its families and children, and was told that you know a good deal about it. May I ask you some questions?" As the consultant asks questions and encourages the informant to talk about the neighborhood, he or she pays particular, if not obvious, attention to names that have recurred in previous interviews. Opinions of the informants may vary as to the helpfulness of these persons, and such opinions should be noted, but the most important criterion at this point is centrality in the network as indicated by multiple nominations. The consultant will also want to analyze what the informants say about families and specific instances of helping behavior for an indication of the local childrearing customs, expectations, and values. It is better to obtain this information indirectly from specific examples. Informants are seldom able to respond usefully to such questions as "Who are the helpers in this neighborhood?" or "What are the general practices concerning leaving children unattended (or spanking them) around here?"

Each neighborhood will have its own list of people to interview, depending on its residential patterns, ethnic background, socioeconomic characteristics, and local institutions. However, a general list might include:

- Local social agency personnel.
- Public health nurses.
- School personnel (secretaries, janitors, and active parents, as well as principals and long-time teachers).
- Clergy.
- Long-time elderly residents.
- Merchants, pharmacists, grocery checkers, and so forth.
- Recreational workers (playgrounds, after-school programs, and organized children's sports programs).

In addition to being sources of information about other natural helpers, some of these people may be natural helpers themselves. Therefore, the door should always be left open for further contacts. It is advisable, however, to limit the initial interview to information gathering and leave recruitment to a later stage.

While visiting local residents in their homes or in various gathering places, while shopping in local stores, eating in restaurants, or attending community meetings and festivities, the consultant should always be looking for clues about the way families live, about how they perceive things, and with whom they interact. Sometimes chance occurrences provide the best information, but the consultant can improve on chance by being around the neighborhood a good deal and by having a clear idea of what kind of information is useful. One consultant, for example, was annoyed at being continually interrupted while he interviewed one potential natural helper. Children were constantly underfoot. The phone rang all the time and other mothers kept dropping by. He finally realized that the "interruptions" were the best data he could gather about how this natural helper functioned. He began to concentrate more on what was happening around him than on answers to specific questions.

Developing a Plan of Action

By the time fieldwork is completed, the consultant should be feeling comfortable in the target neighborhood and should have a great deal of information about families, children, and natural helpers. The consultant may have already witnessed some instances of informal preventive or protective services or have heard about a situation that has a number of people worried. Having spent a considerable period as a learner, the consultant may feel that it is time to "prove" to the agency or to the neighborhood that he or she can actually do something. Direct intervention in the neighborhood at this point is not advisable, however. In some cases, where the consultant wears several other hats, such intervention may be unavoidable. But intervening in a protective role may be especially hard to reconcile with the consultant's supposedly rather detached interest in the workings of the neighborhood. Whenever possible, it would be better for the consultant to be relieved of case responsibility in the target neighborhood. If this is not possible, the consultant will have to explain that, while the protective function is one aspect of the job, he or she is also interested in broader, supportive actions on behalf of families. But there is no easy solution to this problem.

Instead of offering service at this point, the consultant should pause to review the information received. General knowledge of the neighborhood gained from participant observation should help in the evaluation of the persons who have been suggested as natural helpers. What has been learned about their styles of interaction can be compared with neighborhood values and unwritten rules. A supervisor from the agency or some other outside person can help to provide an objective point of view: at this point, the consultant needs a consultant. This outsider can also help to review and revise the goals of the project, which might include any or all of the following:

- Gaining more information about the childrearing culture of the neighborhood.
- Increasing the reporting of cases of child abuse to the proper agencies.
- Diverting borderline cases of abuse or neglect into informal helping systems.
- Strengthening local child-relevant institutions and facilities.
- Developing surveillance and supportive resources for isolated or abusing families.

The selection of goals should be based on specific *neighborhood* needs, not on the needs of the agency. Once a clearer picture of the goals has been developed, the selection of appropriate central figures for further contact can proceed. In addition to their relevance to the goals of the project, central figures can be selected on the basis of the following criteria:

1. *Stability*. Persons who seem to be committed to long-term residence in the neighborhood can be contacted repeatedly

and will be able to pass along the benefits of the consultation program over a longer period of time than transient residents will.

2. *Accessibility.* Some central figures may be more interested in working with the consultant than others, either because they need support or because the consultant is personally compatible.

3. *Direct relevance for child maltreatment.* Some central figures may not have direct access to the families who are most vulnerable to child maltreatment. They may deal mostly with other groups, such as the elderly. While they are important helpers in their networks, they would not be good candidates for this project.

4. *Apparent extent of networks.* All other things being equal (which of course they never are), consultation provided to those central figures with the largest networks will have the greatest impact.

The actual selection process probably will not be nearly so rational or sequential as it has been outlined here. However, this description can serve as a model and guide. In choosing from the names that have been supplied, the consultant can afford to be particular, since he or she will probably not want to provide consultation to more than two or three natural helpers, adding others as he or she gains experience. The better the initial selection process, the greater the payoff of the consultation (no small consideration for a consultant and an agency that are hungry for results). And as mentioned previously, it is much harder to end a relationship with an unproductive helper than to decide not to begin it in the first place. The stage is now set to develop the consultation relationship. Alice Collins describes this relationship in more detail in the following chapter, and in so doing provides some guidelines for cultivating and maintaining it.

CHAPTER 7

Helping Neighbors Intervene in Cases of Maltreatment

Alice H. Collins

The consultation method was developed after mental health practitioners came to recognize that there were not enough mental health professionals to help all the people who had emotional problems. They decided that the best solution was to use such professionals to "work with the people who work with the people." The intention was not to annex these individuals to the mental health professions but to enable them to be more effective in their own roles as teachers, nurses, ministers, correctional staff members, and the like.

The psychiatrists who developed the new approach were influenced by the medical model of treatment in which an attending physician consults with a specialist about the diagnosis and treatment of a patient. In this model, the consultant examines the patient and gives the attending physician his

133

expert findings. The developers of the new approach were also influenced by the public health model, which focuses on preventing illness by creating an environment that has no noxious elements and contributes to health. According to this model, if primary prevention is not possible, then prompt treatment or secondary prevention must be made available. If this effort fails, the tertiary goal is to avoid further deterioration and to maintain as much normal functioning in afflicted individuals as possible.

These ideas led to a set of principles to guide the consultation relationship (Caplan, 1970). Adapted for general use by practitioners in the helping professions, they are:

- To be effective, consultation should be requested by the person who needs help in solving a problem in his or her practice.
- Interviews between consultant and consultee are confidential.
- The consultee is not obliged to follow the advice of the consultant.
- The consultant has no supervisory or administrative connection with the consultee but is rather a partner, knowledgeable in her own field as the consultee is in his.
- A major objective of consultation is to enable the consultee to handle similar problems that may arise in the future without further need for consultation.

These principles are especially useful for professionals who want to make the transition from a one-to-one approach for prevention and treatment to a method designed to reach a large clientele "once removed." We have applied them while working on a project designed for providers and recipients of daycare services (Collins and Watson, 1976). Our experiences in this project have caused us to make some minor adjustments in these principles, but that same experience formed the basis for our subsequent work (Collins and Pancoast, 1976), including the present discussion.

Adapting Consultation to Combat Child Maltreatment

The consultation approach, as applied to child maltreatment, suggests three objectives:

- Primary prevention aims to ensure that the safe, healthy development of children is not stunted by unrealistic parental expectations, violence, or other disruption of normal parent-child relationships.
- Secondary prevention seeks to discover instances of maltreatment at the earliest possible point and to remedy the environmental and interpersonal causes.
- Tertiary treatment aims at separating the child from the abusing adults to prevent injury or death.

Consultants must remember that they will not be working directly with individual perpetrators of child maltreatment, but rather with the central figures in the social networks to which these individuals belong. They will be partners with the natural neighbors in an effort to reduce the incidence and effects of child maltreatment. Becoming a partner may require evaluation of natural neighbors as "experts." Though not professionals in the same sense as teachers or nurses, natural neighbors do have a knowledge of their own networks. This knowledge may be exhaustive, and the central figure's way of functioning, though self-taught, may be no less effective than that of formally trained professionals. Just as teachers understand the hierarchy of the school and methods of class instruction, so natural neighbors understand the intricacies of the relationships within their own networks and the environment around them. They may know, as the professional consultant cannot, what is and what is not possible within their own orbits. Networks are subject to many influences, and consequently each has its idiosyncratic manner of functioning. This being the case, consultants will want to learn all they can about the networks from which they have chosen partners.

Entering the Natural Network

"Choosing a partner" violates the first principle of consultation, namely, that the consultee seek out the consultant for help at the beginning of the partnership. In applying the consultation method to natural networks, however, it becomes clear that it must be the consultant who chooses the target area and takes the initiative in finding and recruiting the natural neigh-bors. It cannot be otherwise since natural neighbors are by defi-nition people who expect to give help, not receive it. They are likely to think of professionals as helping seriously troubled people in offices somewhere, not as working with normal people like themselves at their kitchen tables. Though they may often have wished that they could get advice about difficult problems they have encountered, they generally have no idea that professionals might be a resource for them. Consequently, the consultant must take the first step.

Having found a natural neighbor who appears to be a promising partner in the effort to reduce child maltreatment, the consultant will set out to learn all the neighbor is willing to disclose about the childrearing customs of the network. It should be reemphasized that the first step is to collect as much general information as possible about the network rather than to focus on one of its least attractive aspects, child maltreat-ment. One important outcome of this seemingly very slow ap-proach is that the consultant will collect information that will help distinguish between what he or she sees as child maltreat-ment and what the local culture accepts as responsible childrear-ing practice. While the consultant will have advance knowledge of the reported incidence of maltreatment in the neighborhood, this information probably should not be shared or even men-tioned until the natural neighbor has accepted the consultant as a friend with a specialized interest in and knowledge of human behavior. This first period of acquaintance also will give the consultants an opportunity to reconsider personal attitudes and prejudices as they come closer to accounts of behavior of which they must disapprove. As noted in Chapter Six, this approach will be more difficult for consultants who are at the same time an agency's designated protective services workers.

At first, natural neighbors may well feel that the consul-tant expects them to act as informers to facilitate the apprehen-sion and punishment of offenders. The informer role is inimical to the way natural neighbors view themselves—namely, as peo-ple who help, not people who punish. It would be dishonest for consultants to disclaim responsibility for intervention when a case of maltreatment is referred to their agencies. But they can point out that as partners they wish to share in the natural neighbors' efforts to help all families, including those where maltreatment is a problem. The consultants can draw upon the natural neighbors' special concern with prevention, since, in their official positions, agency-based helpers rarely hear of situations that might be dealt with at an early stage.

Natural neighbors have read and heard many lurid accounts of fatal child maltreatment. They need assistance in resolving the conflict aroused by their knowledge of such conditions and their unwillingness to invade family privacy or to "act as a policeman" and thus trigger painful consequences for a neighbor. In such situations, the consultant needs to support and encourage the natural neighbors but must not take over the final decision for action. The consultant will be most helpful if the natural neighbors are encouraged to discuss the problem, supported by the consultant's sympathetic understanding of the difficult role and the emotion-loaded decisions it entails. The natural neighbors may find their place in the network jeopardized when it becomes known that they have "turned someone in." Nor can the action of a court in a child maltreatment case be firmly predicted. Dismissal of such a case will also change the light in which the network sees a natural neighbor.

Thus, unless a consultant decides that a case involves a life-and-death situation, he or she must make every effort not to "take over" but rather to support and encourage natural neighbors in coming to their own conclusions. This self-control can produce long-range rewards. It is an active demonstration that the consultant is indeed a partner who understands the difficulties of the neighbor role and who will help without taking action that might diminish the natural neighbor as a partner. It will also have the practical advantage of giving both partners time to think through all the possibilities for remedial action *with* rather than *against* the individuals responsible for the maltreatment.

Building Long-Term Protection

The following case* demonstrates how a trusting relationship with a consultant, built up over many visits, encouraged a natural neighbor to initiate legal action aimed at protecting the children of a friend. More direct intervention by official services could not have supported the children as well, both before and after court action.

The consultee, Mrs. Hanes (thirty-four years old but looking considerably older), had known the consultant for six months. She had revealed a good deal about her early life, which had been characterized by neglect. The only stable, loving person she had known was her grandmother, with whom she lived intermittently when her own mother did not require her as a housekeeper and babysitter, tasks she began at age four. She married an older man at fourteen to escape the home and the advances of a series of stepfathers. She divorced him and married a war veteran who was a heavy drinker. She, too, drank heavily until a doctor told her that her miscarriages were due to her alcoholism. She stopped drinking and had a little girl, Carlene, now eight, whom she adores. Even though the family lived at the subsistence level on her husband's veteran's disability payments, Mrs. Hanes was known to her neighbors—and to the community center social workers—as a person who was always ready to help if needed. Her health was not very good, but between bouts of illness she was active in her large network, and she was always interested in how other members of the network were doing. Her home was located in a neighborhood that had been purchased for industrial development. Her house was not overly clean, but it could still be identified by the fence that she had put up to protect Carlene when she was a toddler and that now served the same purpose for the children whom she some-

*The case material quoted hereafter is taken from taped interviews conducted by Eunice L. Watson. It was edited by the author. The work was done as part of the Daycare Exchange Project and the Field Study of the Neighborhood Family Daycare System, Children's Bureau Grants D-135, R-287, Department of Health, Education, and Welfare.

times babysat. It was a neighborhood that would most closely resemble the transitory type described in Chapter Four. She was quickly identified as a natural neighbor and recruited. The consultant found the partnership with her to be a happy and productive one.

9/20/75

Mrs. Hanes: And talk about babysitting. I got in a mess the other night. Carlene was out playing and she runs in and says, "Mama, Aunt June wants you." Now that's Larry and Beverly's mother. And I was doing the dishes and I told her, "Well, you tell her I'll be over as soon as I quit doing the dishes." So I went over and June was sitting there so drunk she couldn't move. And those two kids running around there, Larry smoking cigarettes—he's eight—drinking beer. He was going through her purse and took five dollars and I made him put it back. I sent Carlene to get my husband because I couldn't carry her—you know the doctor said about my back—so he put her in the bed and then I went and got the kids and put them down—Beverly, she's just two—and told them to stay there and I went over two hours later and they were sound asleep. But that was a mess. What in the world is wrong with that woman?

Consultant: She really is sick.

Mrs. Hanes: Well, but to get drunk like that—I've seen drunks, but she was the worst. There's something that's got to be done—those kids are suffering too damn bad.

Consultant: Yes—does this happen often?

Mrs. Hanes: Practically every night, maybe not quite so bad, but she comes home every night after she's stopped at the tavern mostly drunk and men with her and she locks those two kids out of the house or puts them to bed.

Consultant: What happens in the daytime?

Mrs. Hanes: She works at the Sunnyside Nursing Home. But how the hell can she get so drunk and get up and go to work next morning? Seems she's helping the helpless, why can't she help her own children? Can't she see her own children? My house is dirty, I know, sometimes, but a pigpen's cleaner than hers—dirty dishes sitting around and old beer bottles—you got to wade through them.

Consultant: Would you want to call the Protective Division? Or have me call?

Mrs. Hanes: Some of the neighbors did call the police and they came out and they talked to me, but I just couldn't tell them anything. If I had, they would have picked her up—they know I tell the truth—but I just couldn't do it. I thought I'd give her another chance.

Consultant: How many chances can you give her?

Mrs. Hanes: Oh, I know, but I just can't bring myself to do it.

Consultant: It's a hard thing to do.

Mrs. Hanes: Because I know what it would be like if someone took my daughter away. And you know when June's sober she says, "What would I do without you, you're the only one I can depend on." It's like I'd be double-crossing her.

Consultant: Yeah—but let's look at it another way. She knows I come to talk to you and so maybe you could blame it on me. And I will be glad to call the Protective Division or the police if you want me to—but they will need you to make the complaint sometime.

Mrs. Hanes: I do think the responsibility of the kids—it bothers her—lately she sends them over here at night—

Consultant: Maybe she would be relieved to have the kids taken care of?

Mrs. Hanes: I know—but I keep thinking how I'd feel without Carlene.

10/20/75

Mrs. Hanes: You know those kids? Well, I got Mrs. B. to babysit them and she takes awful good care of those kids—she lives right over there. But June still lets them run wild. But Mrs. B. isn't going to keep them because June promised to pay two dollars a day and bring milk and she don't bring the milk and don't pay on time. I don't know what she'll do—ask me probably—but I won't—the doctor said not to 'til my back is all better—

Consultant: Do you think there is any chance of her going along with foster care now?

Mrs. Hanes: No, 'cause I tried to say I'd take them all the time when I'm OK and she says she won't give them up—she says she don't want them but she won't give them up. That's why I can't understand. But they're getting worse —Larry is setting fires and Bev's running around the street until midnight—I'm so scared she'll get run over. Can I have your telephone number so maybe some night I might want you to call the police?

Consultant: Call me any time.

Mrs. Hanes: I don't know why the school doesn't do something —Carlene says Larry is way behind and mostly just sits and doesn't do his work.

Consultant: You wouldn't mind if I talked to the school social worker about him?

Mrs. Hanes: No—maybe they should report it.

The consultant discussed the situation with the school social worker, who said Larry was a slow learner, that his mother made an excellent impression when she came to school, that she expressed concern that she could not manage to make him wash properly and that the school had certainly no grounds for official complaint to a protective agency.

Very upset, Mrs. Hanes phoned the consultant and said a neighbor had called the police to June's house because of the noise and the presence of a succession of men. Mrs. Hanes said two women detectives came and interviewed June, who had been drinking. There was a man at June's and the children were out in the street, but the detectives did not do anything to change things for the children or make June "shape up."

12/13/75

Mrs. Hanes: Why didn't they take them right then? What's the use of calling—just make her mad and don't help the children. They told her to clean up the place so she comes over and gets me to help her and for a few nights she didn't bring no men home and now it's right back where it was.

Consultant: Would you want me to call and find out what the status is?

Mrs. Hanes: Yes, now I would—something has to be done. I really hate to have to say anything but those kids can't suffer any more.

The consultant got in touch with the local protective division worker, who called, warned June to clean up her house and take better care of her children, but did not remove them. Mrs. Hanes was extremely distressed and talked to the consultant bitterly about the lack of concern everyone seemed to feel for the children. The consultant again called the protective division and discussed the situation. Eventually, a date was set for a court hearing.

1/10/76

Mrs. Hanes: June knows they are going to take the kids away. When the cops were there last week, she came over here and jumped all over me and called me a dirty rat and everything else, and I said, "You had it coming, didn't you." And she said, "Yeah, but I didn't think you'd turn me in." "Well," I said, "you know how long I took care of you when you were drunk and looked after the kids and everything."

Mrs. Hanes went on to review the situation and to justify her action. The consultant supported her and pointed out how important a role she had played in saving the children, who were placed in foster care by the court. Both the consultant and Mrs. Hanes continued their interest in June. It might have been easier for Mrs. Hanes to avoid further contact with this troublesome neighbor, but she was sensitive to June as a suffering person and was ready to continue a helping, not a punishing, relationship with her. At the same time, Mrs. Hanes kept in touch with the children because she acknowledged their ties to her.

3/12/76

Consultant: What's happening with June now?

Mrs. Hanes: Well, she's been evicted and she's supposed to get out by April. She's over here telling me her troubles all the time like nothing ever happened.

Consultant: Has she seen the children at all?

Mrs. Hanes: No, she's talked to Beverly on the phone. I called the lady who is taking care of Beverly and we had a nice talk—she says the kids have told her about me. I said any time she wants, to bring them to visit and I think she will when she thinks they've settled down.

4/16/76

Mrs. Hanes: June's daughter came and got her and took her to California. I known her so long and I never knew she had seven older children that all got took away from her! And this daughter is very strict about drink, but the welfare said she had to do something because June was like helpless. I really think June is retarded in her own mind.

Consultant: It's kind of hard to tell whether it's retardation or just so much more emotional strain than she can manage —you know—

Mrs. Hanes: Yeah—she's like one of these people who has to have somebody behind her to push her. Somebody to tell her what to do—to lean on. She made me feel bad, though. She came over here and said, "If it weren't for you I'd have my kids now." I said, "Did I tie your arms and pour whiskey down you and ask all those men over, and let the kids run loose?"

Consultant: Well, it was kind of like when she actually had to leave you, she had to get mad at you so she could leave.

Mrs. Hanes: Yeah, she came back that night and said goodbye to our puppy and Carlene, and she just grabbed me and broke down and bawled and said, "I'm not mad at you and thank you for helping me—and I'll miss you a lot."

Consultant: And she will, too. Well, that's a good end to that chapter.

Mrs. Hanes: Unless she comes back!

Here, Mrs. Hanes demonstrated an understanding of June, based on her past experiences, that the consultant did not have.

10/3/76

Mrs. Hanes: I got a phone call from June the other day—she says she's getting along fine but she thinks she'll come back to town. I just said, "Heavens, stay where you are, kid." The way she talked she wants to get the kids back. But she says she guesses there's no chance 'til they're old enough to come to her by themselves. And you know they won't, but I just said, "That's right, that's fine, you just stay where you are and have a good time." Because the kids call me and they been to visit and they like it fine in the foster home and they never even mentioned her. And June said, "I guess you're right—I'm better off without them." And that made me feel better 'cause I always had a guilty complex there. We talked a long time but I'm sure she'll stay away from the kids OK.

These excerpts are quoted from a record of almost two thousand typed pages and give only a small indication of the scenes the natural neighbor reported to the consultant. The consultant's patience unquestionably contributed to resolving the situation. But she also closely adhered to the consultation principles noted earlier. She accepted the problem as Mrs. Hanes presented it. She did not assume either a supervisory role or a therapist's role but carefully maintained a relation of partnership, keeping confidentiality until Mrs. Hanes released her from it. It is also obvious that time-limited meetings would not have sufficed to build this kind of constructive relationship. Finally, the experience will probably embolden the natural neighbor to act with greater promptness in another such situation as a result of her new picture of herself.

Taking Action Consistent with Neighborhood Standards

In other cases of serious neglect, the natural neighbor's actions may be much more direct and much less in accordance with the consultant's concept of good practice than were Mrs.

Hanes'. When dictated by a culture and personality that differ substantially from those of the professional, such actions may tax the consultant's capacity for acceptance. Hence, the consultant will do well to remember that, without the natural neighbor's unorthodox approach, preventive intervention in the following example would not have been possible at all.

Mrs. Earl was the manager of a trailer court, a rather grandiose name for the collection of tiny one- and two-bedroom units at the edge of town in a neighborhood known for its high incidence of petty crime and disorderly conduct. In this case, the consultant chose the neighborhood because of its reportedly high rate of child neglect. She had previously developed a relationship with the supervisor and staff of the welfare agency in the community, and it was agreed that the agency would continue to maintain contact with the natural neighbors after funds for research ran out.

The welfare office was somewhat dismayed when the consultant announced that a study of the neighborhood strongly suggested that Mrs. Earl be chosen as natural neighbor. Mrs. Earl was all too well known to the agency. She had twelve children. Her husband was a seasonal worker. The "managership" of the trailer court provided only a house for her family, so in the winter months she often needed welfare assistance herself and loudly demanded every available service. She also constantly phoned the agency, complaining either that a resident of the trailer court was working and so was using aid illegally or that help was not given promptly enough to others. She had the home telephone numbers of the staff and did not hesitate to call at night.

Although she was always very short of money, she used her first month's check of twenty-five dollars (paid to all natural neighbors in the research project as a token of gratitude for their investment of time in talking to the consultants) to run an advertisement in the community paper announcing that she was a daycare neighbor and would help make family daycare arrangements for givers and users.

10/14/74

Mrs. Earl: Have a couple here from Arkansas—Don and Juanita —he works in the S Street laundry and I bet he makes between $100 and $140 a week. The woman and the kids went barefooted—never had no clothes—and what groceries—she never went to the store—he'd go buy a couple little bags of groceries once a week and that's all they had to live on and they've got four kids and the baby only five months old. Some people in the court told me they knew those little kids hadn't had anything to eat for three days and that made me kind of mad because I don't believe in doing kids that way. So I went down and I talked to her and I said, "Look, I don't care what you do with your husband, but," I said, "either you change your ways about these kids—they're going to eat and eat right —or I'm going to turn you in and have them put in a place where they can be taken care of properly." I said, "Juanita, I know you love your kids but you'd better love them more than you love that man." And she said, "But I'm scared of him, he beats me."

So she got to talking and she told me she had left him in Arkansas and the welfare made her go back to him because they said, "Either go back to him or do without because we won't give you anything—nothing." She went back. And he told her if she left him he'd take the kids and she'd be just on her own—and she'd had very little schooling—in her early twenties and four bitty children under four. He said she couldn't get no help or nothing. So I told her, "Honey, he's wrong. You could get welfare and live a lot better." So they told me he come in last Friday and he beat her—he had his money, $142, and he spent $23 on groceries—Brenda lives next door told me and she went and got Juanita and the kids when he left and fed them all, and then Don come in and Juanita asked him to go get some milk for those kids. And he said, "The hell with you. I need that money and I ain't throwing it away on you and the kids."

And Brenda said those kids were just crying and shaking they was so hungry, so she went and got some milk but she can't do that much—she has a family of her own—so she came over and asked me, "Do you know any welfare people where Juanita could get in?" I said, "Yeah." I know most of them up there—so Brenda said, "Will you take her up?" and I said, "Well, I can't right now"—my husband was here—he says don't interfere in family affairs. So I told her, "You got to call and make an appointment, because there's no sense in just going up there without talking to nobody, because you won't get nowhere." So my husband say, "You're not interfering." He was going hunting with these friends of ours. So then I called her to come up here and call. She called and they put her off 'til Monday. And those little kids, honest to God, didn't have nothing, no milk, no nothing. And he beat her up. So—I was interested in getting food for the babies; so, being that she had already called, I said, "You call them here again." And she called and she talked—and I said, "Now don't lie to 'em, tell 'em the truth. If you want to go to them, go all the way and tell 'em the truth." So she told 'em the truth, how he beat her, how the little kids didn't have nothing to eat, and I talked to the woman then that she was talking to, you know, and I told 'em who I was. And I said, "Now I don't care what you do, this is none of my affair, but," I said, "I'm interested in these little kids and that's what you're there for," and, I said, "These little kids need food now, not Monday." I said, "I have eight kids of my own here and I can't afford to feed 'em, nor all the neighbors can't." So the welfare woman says, "Can't you bring her up? If you come up and get these papers and then if you bring her personally at nine o'clock tomorrow morning, I'll talk to you a minute and take care of her."

So I took her up and got the papers and I said, "Will you call and see that she can get surplus foods, you know, the commodities, because for babies they do give a case of milk," and I said, "This baby needs milk. Those little boys and girls has not even had a half a gallon of milk in the last three months among them. It's awful!" So they helped me to get the arrangements made so she could get commodities, and I took her up and got her commodities, and I let her stay here. My brother-in-law come up and knew she was here, and my brother-in-law had been drinking with her husband. So he went down and let him know where she was at. So I slipped her out the back door and slipped her into a cabin down where a single girl's living, and she stayed with her. She stayed in there day and night. Wouldn't open the curtains, you know. And I'd go in and talk to her, you know.

This rush of words was characteristic of Mrs. Earl and many other natural neighbors. It was essential that the consultant try to understand what was being described without interrupting for explanations. Questioning might well have led Mrs. Earl to classify the consultant as a critical interrupter. Mrs. Earl had known many professionals in that role, which seemed inquisitorial to her. It is likely that she had not previously met someone who *listened* with tacit acceptance of her account of events. The consultant's sympathetic attitude established the relationship of trust essential for the partnership.

11/2/74

Mrs. Earl: The little kids don't have a toy of no kind. Nothing! And it's pitiful. This man's making good money and out drinking and running around. I knew he'd have that other woman there all the time. His rent was paid till the twenty-sixth and I knew he'd have her in here the whole time and it'd be nothing but misery for everybody and it was really hurting Juanita. So I gave him two weeks rent back and told him to get out. And he says, "I will tonight." And I says, "You'll get out in one hour or I'll have the law come and escort you out, but when they do they'll escort you to jail where you belong." And I left and when I come back, he was gone. But he didn't know that she's in the court here. He surmises that she's here somewhere—   ·

Consultant: Oh, he doesn't know where—

Mrs. Earl: He doesn't know where she is—no. Don't dare let him know because he beats her up terrible. And he's mean to the little kids.

Consultant: Doesn't welfare have to try to get support money from him, so that—

Mrs. Earl: The welfare told her they're not going to let him know where she's at. They're going to let him know that she's on welfare, and she has signed papers [so] that the support money comes to the D.A.'s office through the county clerk and back to the welfare. It don't come to her at all. Well, this will get him because he figures if he pays support he can bring it right to her, you know, and give him an excuse to get to her. But the welfare said they're not going to let him know where she's at, at all. She goes up tomorrow morning at nine o'clock to the D.A.'s and signs papers—in court.

12/7/74

Mrs. Earl: I told her, "I wouldn't let him get the best of me." See, she told me she left him and was gone three months and he talked her into going back to him, and she wasn't back to him no time 'til he just beat the holy hell out of her—

Consultant: Is that right?

Mrs. Earl: —just beat her terrible, and she's always been ascared of him. I told her, I says, "I wouldn't let him get to me. I would make him understand that he is the father of the kids and you won't stop him from seeing the kids, as long as he keeps, you know, his place. But if he wants to have a house to live in, he has to pay rent on it." He's always begging her, "Will you go back to me?" And she finally told him, "I'd go back to you, if you could prove your-self a man and take care of the family." But he can't do it. He cannot leave the drink alone and the women. But she herself, you know, is doing real good. I mean—any-body gets disgusted with a woman by themselves, you know, at times.

Consultant: Uh-huh.

Mrs. Earl: But I overlook it, because I know the mistakes I've made when I was younger. I know how lonely a woman can get by herself. And I mean you can get really upset being alone all the time. Never no place to go or nothing to do. So all I do is try to help her and do what I can to give her encouragement. She comes over here quite a bit and sits. But I think she does pretty good for herself. She's learning the hard way.

Consultant: But even if she can't say so, you are certainly help-ing her a lot.

Mrs. Earl: She'll put all her love on them kids, but when they grow older, how is she going to explain—"No, your daddy's not here." Well, boys need a father to have companionship with, and it makes it awful hard. I just—I don't see in stepfathers, I don't see in stepmothers, but still these young people before they have—if they have one child and see they're not going to make it and argue and fuss, they ought to leave each other right then instead of waiting and having more kids and more kids, and then—uh—here she's got four kids here, and now she's left—and had no schooling or nothing else.

Consultant: Yes, it would certainly be better if they could be together—do you think it might work if you talked to Don about it?

Mrs. Earl: I tried that—and all he does is come over here drunk and noisy and breaks in and all. He's driving with no driver's license. He's dog drunk, stays dog drunk, and they will not pick him up. He stands out there and he cusses a blue streak, he cusses everybody, he wants to fight everybody and—I don't know—I can't understand why they won't pick him up.

I told the sheriff—the sheriff that come out last night—I gave him the license number of the car, the description of the car. I told him that Don didn't have no driver's license. I says, "Now, if somebody don't do something about it, I will. I said I've got a gun and I'll shoot it if I have to. I'm not going to put up with drunks in here and losing all my tenants because of the drunks coming in and breaking in." And he says, "I'll take over." He says, "The minute you call, I'll be right here." But then Don didn't come back, drove in and right back out.

But I've got a trap set for him. I've got her light on. Up to now we've had her door locked and the light off. Well, I've got her light on. And I think tonight I'm going to leave the lock off her door and I'm going to fix some way on the inside, you know, lock it shut and get out. I don't know what I'll do for sure yet. Then he'll go up there insisting she's there, you know, when he don't see the padlock on the door. I might fool him that way.

Consultant: Mmmm—

Mrs. Earl: What I ought to do is go in there with my gun and stay.

Consultant: Yeah—well, you ought not to do that.

Mrs. Earl: To go in with my gun and say it's my house and if they go in there and start breaking in, shoot at their feet.

Consultant: Yeah—but then you'd get yourself into all sorts of difficulty. There's no point in that.

Whether or not Mrs. Earl was serious about her plan, the consultant responds as though she were. The consultant thus demonstrates concern for Mrs. Earl's welfare and sets some limits for her. The consultant's response violates the consultation model's prohibition against assuming responsibility for the consultee's action, but it also illustrates that this principle must be set aside when a real danger is involved.

1/20/75

Mrs. Earl: Juanita's husband called the welfare Friday and he got very boisterous and loud—Mrs. Woodrum, she told him to come in Monday. And he said, "Well, I'm going on a new job Monday, I'm starting a new job and I work from seven to half-past three." At ten o'clock yesterday morning he was sitting out here at the corner, waiting, watching, trying to find Juanita.

Don found out where Juanita was babysitting and he called her up. And he says, "Now don't hang up, I want to talk to you." She says, "Well, talk away." And he started begging her—"Do you love me?" She says, "No." "Will you go back to me?" She said, "No." "Will you consider it?" She says, "Oh, I'll think about it." "Can I see my kids?" She says, "When the welfare says you can." So he hung up—he got mad and started cussing and everything and he hung up. She asked me what to do, and I said I'd call the caseworker and tell her. Let her know everything that's going on. So the caseworker told her, "If you can find out anything, you know where to get in touch with me."

Scenes like this were repeated many times. The consultant allowed Mrs. Earl to talk freely. This seemed to be her way of reassuring herself that she was doing what was right for the family. Moreover, it helped her deal with being constantly torn by her own memories—memories that were reactivated by Juanita and the children. The consultant had listened to Mrs. Earl's accounts of her miserable and brutalized past but avoided referring to it or attempting to suggest to Mrs. Earl why she was so particularly involved with Juanita.

2/20/75

Mrs. Earl: Last Sunday a week ago Don come out just fine, real gentlemanlike, was just good as could be. He brought a sack of candy for each one of the kids. Then that wasn't enough. She let him take the kids to the store and he went up and bought 'em more candy and ice cream, brought 'em right back. At four o'clock she told him he had to leave and he left, just as nice as could be. Then come along Tuesday he called the welfare, "Is there any way I can have her check cut off? If I have her check cut off, she has to come back to me." Mrs. McCaff says, "No. I'm sorry, there isn't." And I guess he started raising holy thunder with the welfare. Then he came out here and he cussed us, he cussed everybody here—oh the names he called 'em was pitiful.

Consultant: It's good to have Mrs. McCaff back you up, isn't it?

Mrs. Earl: Yeah, the welfare has really been good now they know I am a daycare neighbor.

3/10/75

Mrs. Earl: Juanita asked her caseworker about going to school. But I don't think she should go to school yet. I think the main thing the welfare could give her is more help in getting somebody to teach her to drive and letting her get her a cheap old car. That's all she wants is to get away from that house a little bit. You know a woman can't stand being tied in with four kids and never get out of the house for nothing. And this is the only thing that hurts Juanita. She can't get out of the house for nothing. And of course he's been coming on Sunday. He gets 'em out of bed at half-past seven or eight o'clock in the morning. The kids don't get their complete night's rest. He'll stay there all day long. He had the nerve a week ago to ask her, "You just got your check, didn't you?" She said, "Yes." "Well, how about giving me enough money to pay my rent?" I said, "Girl, don't you give him one penny."

Consultant: Does she do it?

Mrs. Earl: No. She did for the first time or two, and I said, "I wouldn't." Well, I think the main thing that she wants is to go to school. She wants to try to make something of her life. She intends to. She knows that it'll take a long hard time to get through, but, see, the reason she wants to get occupied is because her family wants her to come back to Arkansas, and if she goes back there, Don's family is all back there, and she don't want to be around 'em now. And I think this is why she wants to get occupied into school so that when they say go, she can say, "No, I'm going to school, I can't." I think she's used a little sense in trying to figure out ahead, so that she don't want to hurt none of the family, but she wants to watch for the kids' welfare so that he's not going to come and bother her. And once they get her back there, why then they'd all be around her, and she knows they want him.

Consultant: Hmmm—Well—I do agree with you—she's done wonderfully and you've helped her stand on her own feet.

Mrs. Earl: Yes, I don't want to push her too much, but that's why I told her I was going to leave it up to the case worker.

Consultant: Uh-huh—

Mrs. Earl: But when she mentioned that she was more or less tired of just sitting at home. And she's scared to go out. Now she's had chances to go out with single people, people that don't know him or he don't know, but she won't go because she's scared that he'll find out and take the kids while she's gone.

These abstracts from the five hundred pages of the "Juanita Story" demonstrate how a natural neighbor can intervene at every preventive level and include each actor, from the baby to the father. In the highly unlikely event that professionals had learned of the condition of the children, they certainly could not have proceeded to protect them as Mrs. Earl was able to do. It is predictable that, at the first hint of official interference, Don would simply have "moved on" in the pattern of constant moves that had brought the family from Arkansas to the Pacific Northwest.

The consultant demonstrated her understanding of Mrs. Earl's "take-over" character and her personal style of asking for advice. She did this when she "permitted" Mrs. Earl to chronicle events over and over again. (Much repetitious material has been omitted to spare the reader.) The consultant recognized that this helped Mrs. Earl reassure herself that she was acting correctly. It is interesting to note how Mrs. Earl mobilized the network to protect Juanita and how well she worked with the agency staff, once her own status was accepted by them. No doubt, the earlier efforts of the consultant had smoothed the path toward this desirable end. Other families in need of help will certainly profit from the new mutual respect between the agency and Mrs. Earl.

Until she reviewed the case, the consultant might have wondered whether the many hours spent listening to Mrs. Earl had been time well invested. If nothing else, however, the consultant had learned a great deal about the day-to-day reality of life in a trailer court, an environment she could not otherwise have come to know so intimately. But she had also supported Mrs. Earl's efforts on behalf of the family and had improved her status with the professionals just by her willingness to listen.

Both June and Don appear to fit into the category of dangerously abusive parents. But it is also clear that they can be helped toward a permanently improved life. The partnership approach would seem to be a more humane and more enduring approach than official action that breaks all family ties only after grave maltreatment has occurred. There is no doubt that this approach requires a great deal of patience and flexibility on the part of the professional, an investment for which there are not always commensurate rewards. However, this is no less true of many other situations with which professionals deal.

Taking Early Preventive Action

Cases of gross neglect or abuse are usually the first the consultant hears about because they are the most distressing to the natural neighbors, who feel anxious to intervene but have known or fear the kind of rejection that Mrs. Earl experienced. There are, however, many other less spectacular but no less important instances when the professional can encourage intervention at an early stage. This might involve encouraging parents to gain a better understanding of normal child development and thus to avoid unreasonable expectations about their children. Natural neighbors do often talk about these less drastic situations and ask for reassurance in their customary indirect way. In the following example, the consultant encouraged the natural neighbor to call on network support in coming to the aid of two children.

10/5/72

Mrs. Burns: People are sure funny. My neighbor [Donna] has been taking care of two little boys. Their mother works as a nurse at the hospital and she brings them on her way. Nice little kids—well mannered. You could see they hadn't been mistreated or anything. Once in a while I'd go stay with them if Donna had to go to the doctor or something. But I thought it was kind of funny—when their mother came, she didn't ask any questions why I was there—just said "Come on" to the kids and they acted sort of as though they hardly knew her—good, and did what she said, but not running up to her or crying or the kind of things you'd expect.

Consultant: That does seem strange in such young kids. I wonder why?

Mrs. Burns: She don't talk much to Donna—just drops the kids and drives on in the morning and picks them up at night—

never stays for a cup of coffee or nothing the way most
do. Donna doesn't mind as long as she pays on time, but
it don't seem just right—I don't think there is a father
there either.

Consultant: Would there be any way of getting to know her a
little better and maybe get her into some things with
other parents and kids—does it seem like she might just
be pretty lonesome and sort of cut off?

Mrs. Burns: Well, it really isn't any of my business, but she
doesn't live too far—right next to the shopping center—
maybe I could get Donna to kind of drop in sometime—
though she might be shy to do that—

Consultant: But Donna depends on you a lot and maybe you
could suggest you go with her? They do have that single
parents' club at the Y don't they?

Mrs. Burns had come to the attention of the consultant
because she had called the daycare information and referral center to ask for help in finding good daycare for the "darling"
children for whom she had been caring over the past two years.
Both parents were busy doctors, and she wanted to help them
find good care for their children. Suggestions were made, and
she called again on several occasions on behalf of friends who
wanted to give daycare as well as use it. Since she seemed to be
acting as a natural neighbor, she was recruited to meet with the
consultant. To everyone's regret, she and her family had to
move to a development project in an area beyond that served by
the consultant. But three months later, Mrs. Burns phoned to
say that she had moved again, this time into a large apartment
house in an area resembling the parochial neighborhoods described in Chapter Four, and would be delighted to resume the
relationship. The consultant privately doubted if Mrs. Burns
could become a natural neighbor so quickly in this new environment, but her doubts were swept away at her first visit to the
new apartment. Not only did Mrs. Burns know something about
each of the 100 families that lived there, but people were turning to her for all kinds of help and advice, from childcare to
marital difficulties. She gave such help and advice freely, consid-

ering herself an expert since she had been married three times and had three sets of children. She occasionally mentioned professionals who had helped her and seemed to identify with them, although she saw the consultant less as a professional than as a friend and partner, as indicated by her invitation to the consultant to attend a Tupperware party she was giving.

One of the young women who lived in the apartment house and was attending a community college asked Mrs. Burns if she would babysit the child of some young friends who were both in college. These parents had planned to alternate taking care of the baby, but their schedules would not permit this. Mrs. Burns did not really want another full-time babysitting job since she was already looking after two children of a neighbor across the hall who was a cocktail waitress, but she agreed to take the baby on a part-time basis.

4/26/73

Mrs. Burns: I've got that Ainsworth baby now—in fact, she's asleep in the bedroom this minute. She's a real doll.

Consultant: How does Peggy get along with her? [Peggy is Mrs. Burns' three-year-old.]

Mrs. Burns: Well, for the first couple of days not so good. But she's learning now she can't be rough with the baby. I told Jean Ainsworth when I first took the baby that I had a little one, too, you know, and I said, "I wouldn't let her deliberately hurt the baby but I can't exactly stand and watch her every minute." And that was fine with the Ainsworth kids because they planned on having some more too, and they think it's good for Mimi to get used to it—but of course she's way too little for that. Mae downstairs—she's mad at me because she wanted to baby-sit [Mimi] and I didn't send them to her. Mae, she's the one was working and only paying $2.50 for her two kids so she couldn't get a sitter and now she's staying home and wants me to find her some kids to sit for. And I told her, "Please stay off my back." I'm not going to send her babies. She loves her own kids, she's got her whole life built around them. Everybody has to give in to them. She'd feed and dry a baby but that would be it, you

know. And babies need loving most. They got to have it.
I just don't think she's the kind could love someone else's
baby.

This is a good illustration of the ability and willingness of
natural neighbors to make personality judgments based on daily
observation and acquaintance and to act accordingly. So subtle
an evaluation would be almost impossible for an office-based
professional to make.

5/4/73

Mrs. Burns: The Ainsworth baby is here from eight to five
usually, unless they change up there at the school sometimes. I can always tell when daddy brings her. Her diaper's on like you'd never believe it. Her hat's crooked.
He's a nervous wreck from taking care of her and he just
hands her to me. I don't think that kid is twenty-one because once we were talking about teenagers and he says,
"That's us, too, you know." But they were like a lot of
others who've come here—they want care for the baby
and they don't care a bit about licenses or anything, they
don't want to listen to any rules or nothing. All they care
about is finding somebody good to take care of the baby
right away. In fact, when they called me it was about
seven or eight in the morning and they brought the baby
at eleven and took off.

Consultant: I think the social worker at the nursery where they
applied first said he [the father] was taking the baby to
school with him before that.

Mrs. Burns telephoned to tell the consultant that she was
going to be away for a time because her mother was in the hospital. She had made arrangements with reliable people in the
apartment house to care for the children she was babysitting.
But she had told the Ainsworths to find another sitter. Mrs.
Burns was annoyed because they often failed to let her know
when they were not coming and also because they had a fairly
large unpaid bill, and this seemed an amicable way of terminat-
ing the arrangement. After she got home, Mike Ainsworth came,
paid the past bill, and begged Mrs. Burns to take the baby back.

9/12/73

Mrs. Burns: My husband said this phone was hot constantly while I was gone. There was either Mike or Jean wanting me. The last Saturday I was gone he said they called four times. So when I got back I wondered what in the world was wrong, so I called them and they said would I take her for a few days because they had some business they had to do and they didn't want to try to find another babysitter. So of course I said yes and I've still got her. I'd bet you a million dollars that business stuff was just to get me to take her again and it's been going ever since.

Consultant: They bring diapers and things?

Mrs. Burns: Never enough. I used to put some of my old stuff on her and save the one to go home in—but that was no good so I told Jean, "A baby needs a lot of diapers." She says, "Why can't you train her?" And I keep telling her, "This is a baby—she acts like she's supposed to act—don't expect her to be all grown up." And now she's beginning to walk and get into things they are forever slapping her hands and stuff. It aggravates me so, I think I'll let her go. (Mimi wakes and comes in, climbs onto Mrs. Burns' lap.)

Consultant: She is so cute! (Mike comes in, is introduced to consultant.) You sure have a cute little girl.

Mike: Thank you.

Consultant: Are you back at school again now?

Mike: Yeah—in both senses. I'm working at the high school and back at college. I'm a teacher's aide.

Mrs. Burns: (To M.) That's beef and noodles in that jar. She just woke up so she wasn't ready to eat but she may be hungry by the time you get her home. And here are her sweater and pants. It got hot so I took them off and she doesn't need them now but it'll be cool tomorrow morning. You going to bring her Saturday or not?

Mike: No, I'll take her with me to Middletown.

Mrs. Burns: Get her shoes, will you?

Mike: I hope so—

Mrs. Burns: (To consultant) Mimi put her shoes in the toilet or the bathtub one night and made Jean so mad she couldn't see straight. She was telling me, all frustrated, and said she wasn't going to get her new ones, just so she'd remember not to do it again. I said, "It didn't surprise me—she's just at that age where water—and she's still too little to remember—you just have to watch her. But I'm glad you're getting some because she can walk outdoors now when it's nice, instead of sitting in the stroller."

The Ainsworths were obviously learning how to be parents from Mrs. Burns, and she, in turn, was getting approval and reinforcement from the consultant. That relationship undoubtedly helped her to weather a serious breach with the network that occurred shortly thereafter.

Several people in the apartment house had made a point of telling Mrs. Burns that they thought she ought to "do something" about a new family that had recently moved in. The family members had made no contacts with other families. In fact, the father left for work early and did not exchange the customary greetings with other workbound men, and the mother was rarely seen except perhaps during a quick trip to empty the garbage can. She did her laundry at night when the laundry room was usually empty. There were sounds of a child screaming whenever one passed the door and the voice of a child begging to be "let loose." Network members reminded Mrs. Burns that she was connected with the consultant, so why didn't she do something? She felt it her duty and did knock on the door several times without result except to hear the mother sternly whispering to the child to be quiet. On one occasion, she waited for the mother to go out at her usual time with the garbage, peeked in, and saw a small boy tied to the bed. She had never seen him outdoors and was shocked and upset. She immediately reported it to the Children's Services, which sent a caseworker to question others in the building. To Mrs. Burns' surprise, her neighbors were extremely critical of her and berated her for "getting them into it" and putting them in danger of retaliation by the family. It was a most bewildering experience for the natural neighbor, who reported the incident to the con-

sultant, saying that she was not going to continue the partnership since it had gotten her into so much trouble. The consultant agreed that sometimes the role of natural neighbor did
involve trouble but was able to help Mrs. Burns see that the protection of the children was more important than the network's
temporary ill will—a sentiment that did, in fact, gradually
diminish.

It cannot be stressed too much that the consultant should
avoid labeling the kind of behavior described above as neglectful, even though both consultant and natural neighbor know
that technically it is. The implications of wilful injury to children are very ugly and hard to remove. It is easier for everyone
concerned if neglectful behavior is viewed and discussed as evidence of immaturity and inexperience so that, when it is cor-
rected, no stigma remains. Care must also be taken to avoid
judgments before the situation is completely understood.

Combating Maltreatment in a Privileged Neighborhood

Maltreatment occurs even where poverty is not a problem. Outward physical conditions, in fact, may appear very
comfortable and even luxurious. In these circumstances children
actually may have fewer safeguards from society than do poor
children. A school nurse or principal is less likely to call on
parents living in a $75,000 home than on parents living in a
ghetto apartment to discuss the severely bruised appearance of a
child. Even if such maltreatment is reported to the appropriate
agency, it is less likely that action will be taken to protect the
children in the future. While there are more parent education
groups and courses open to parents with leisure, few of those
who maltreat their children will spontaneously attend. And, although parents may be involved in a complicated set of interactions with "society," they still may be emotionally isolated.
Again, they have the means to purchase the physical isolation
not available to poor parents. This underlines the need to identify and recruit natural neighbors in middle- and upper-class
neighborhoods as well as in poor ones. Natural neighbors can be
found in affluent areas, although the informants may be a little

less ready to talk with the consultant than are those living in poorer areas. However, there are other ways of finding natural neighbors. One can explore the boards of directors of organizations concerned with family welfare, of cultural programs such as junior art, and of symphony programs or volunteer school tutoring programs.

Mrs. Towne was chosen as a natural neighbor for a number of reasons. She did not fit the stereotype of family daycare giver. She lived in a fashionable suburb, the kind characterized as integral in Chapter Four. Her husband owned a successful business, and they had two children in a private elementary school. She had shown exceptional interest and understanding of the daycare neighbor concept when it was explained to the board of the community center where she was a member. At the first interview, it was discovered that for years she had taken care of the child (Lena) of a working friend after school and on Saturdays. She had a busy social life and a large circle of friends that formed a network across a wide area. At a dinner party, one of the men complained that he was about to lose the best secretary he had had in years because she couldn't find a babysitter, and he couldn't see any sense in supporting United Way day nurseries if they couldn't even find a place for this kid. It turned out that Terry, the little girl in question, was six years old and therefore not eligible for day nursery care, but attended kindergarten only half a day. Mrs. Towne volunteered to try to find care for her. She reported the whole incident to the consultant.

9/12/72

Mrs. Towne: You know, I've asked my old friend Patty to take several kids but she hasn't wanted to. There's always been something else. But this time we were at bridge club and I mentioned it to Della because she has a six-year-old, too, and it seemed as though it ought to work out, but she kind of hemmed and hawed. Quick as a flash, Patty said she'd take her! It's just right because Mrs. Dodge, Terry's mother, had called me—Joe [Mrs. Dodge's employer] had told her to—and her own mother is just about to leave— she used to babysit—and she wants a place Terry can come alone and Patty lives across from the school. So Patty said, "Tell the mother to come down and see me," and I did and it's all fixed! The mother is real young and very pretty and divorced—doesn't it seem like all of them are.

10/15/72

Consultant: How is Terry getting on?

Mrs. Towne: Patty says she's the nicest little girl, but she sure needs a lot of attention. She says the first week she just followed her around all day. She said, "When I baked a pie it just fascinated her and I let her bake a little one to take home," but Terry said, "I can eat it right here—my mother doesn't eat things like that because she wants to stay thin."

Consultant: Patty and Mrs. Dodge get along fine, too?

Mrs. Towne: She stopped and talked the first few nights when she picked Terry up, Patty said, but now she just honks her horn or calls up and says for Terry to walk home and she'll meet her there because she has to work late. Patty worries about it—she doesn't think that's right.

Consultant: It's so good that you can help her understand how different the situation is from when she was raising her own kids. When Patty can tell you about little things that bother her, she's going to be able to go back and handle them better than if she had to bottle it all up inside.

Mrs. Towne: Well, Patty isn't the kind that bottles things up, but I do think it helps her to talk because she knows now that I have Lena and she asks me about little things I wouldn't have thought she would because she's raised her own kids.

12/16/72

Mrs. Towne: Patty is worried because Mrs. Dodge hasn't paid her in a month. She keeps making excuses but she hasn't paid. And she asked Patty over to see her apartment and Patty says it's beautiful, but she's afraid Mrs. Dodge is getting herself into debt pretty deep. She loves Terry, but she seems to be coming earlier all the time. Patty didn't arrange to give her breakfast but she comes almost every morning just as they are having theirs and Patty asks her, "Did you have breakfast?" and she says, "No," so of course Patty gives it to her. She doesn't mind, of course, but she thinks it is kind of neglecting of Mrs. Dodge not to see that the child eats a good meal before school.

And Mrs. Dodge kind of forgets things. Patty told her a long time ahead she should make arrangements for Terry over the holidays because they always go away, but the night before Mrs. Dodge acted surprised and sort of angry at Patty when she mentioned she wouldn't see Terry for a week. And Patty says something peculiar is going on because Terry never talked about her daddy, but now all of a sudden she is talking about one living there. Patty doesn't think that sounds so good. And Terry is playing a lot of house with the little boy next door—who are you sleeping with and like that. Well, Patty isn't a prude but she doesn't think a little girl should be exposed to all that at home. I said, "Patty, if you don't want them playing that, just break it up."

Consultant: Has she seen any more of Terry's mother?

Mrs. Towne: No, she says Mrs. Dodge isn't a bit friendly. And Patty doesn't think she'll keep Terry in the summer.

Consultant: But I'll bet with your encouragement she will, and it must mean such a lot for Terry.

Mrs. Towne: Well, I can try to talk her into it. I do think it would be awfully hard for Terry and I wouldn't be surprised if Mrs. Dodge just left her alone after school. She is always behind on her payments and she could save money that way.

1/10/73

Mrs. Towne: Patty is really serious about letting Terry go and her husband wants her to, because she gets so upset.

Consultant: With Terry?

Mrs. Towne: Oh no, she says Terry is fine—learning how to behave like a lady and has a lot of friends and all. It's more the home. What really upset Patty was Terry said Dick wasn't there anymore because he spends part of his time with his wife. Patty said, "How can I teach her what's right if this is what's happening at home?" And then Terry has been dawdling later and later about going home —and she oughtn't really to walk all that way when it's so wet and dark out now—and finally one day she said she didn't want to go home because mostly her mother isn't there or just gives her some supper and goes out and tells her she can listen to TV till nine o'clock and then go to bed and if she needs anything, call the superintendent of the building. Terry says she's scared of him because he "acts funny" but she won't say any more. Patty is just awfully upset about it.

Consultant: Has Patty talked about it to Mrs. Dodge?

Mrs. Towne: Well, she says she would, only she hardly ever sees her and it's kind of a hard thing to do without getting Terry into a lot of trouble.

Consultant: Well, you know one of the other natural neighbors was telling me she had a situation something like that. She gets mad pretty easy so she told the mother off and then felt bad because she thought she'd take it out on the child and she'd never come back. But it didn't work out that way. The mother sure was mad, but she changed and things are a lot better.

Mrs. Towne: Well—maybe I could—because, really, the only way Terry knows what is a good family life so she can make one for her own kids is at Patty's. Maybe I can tell her that.

To quote the success of someone in a similar situation rather than to make a direct suggestion often is a good technique. Considerable skill is required, however, not to seem to be making derogatory comparisons. While the word *gossip* often has negative connotations, it is sometimes a useful style of conversation in the consultation relationship.

Improving the Natural Neighbor's Rapport with Other Agencies

The consultant's role in establishing connections between natural neighbors and agencies has been mentioned in some of the cases presented in this chapter. There are times when the consultant is in a position to observe the negative consequences of agency practices. How these should be brought to the attention of the agency must, of course, depend on many factors, including the preferences and relationships of the natural neighbor and the family involved and the professional rapport between agencies. The situation described below illustrates some of the difficulties of being the bridge between agency and natural helper. In this situation, the consultant was confronted with an agency that, in its planning for the client, failed to consider her immaturity and her need for strong support and parent education for the demanding role of working single parent.

Mrs. Prince, who was the manager of an apartment building and whose live-in mother cared for several children, was originally selected for research into family daycare because she seemed to know much neighborhood gossip and to be anxious to impart it. It was not thought that she would fit the standards for a natural neighbor but rather that she could, at the very beginning of the research, provide needed information about her community. The neighborhood included a high proportion of single professional women living with their children in large old houses similar to the one Mrs. Prince managed, either in single-room apartments or in two rooms shared with a friend.

By the time the natural network program had begun, Mrs. Prince's mother had begun receiving Social Security payments and had given up babysitting. When visited, Mrs. Prince told the consultant a great deal about her own difficult life with an irresponsible husband, two teenagers, and a retarded daughter. At every visit, she also described in minute detail the activity of Dolores, who rented the single room across from Mrs. Prince. Dolores was eighteen, had finished high school in an institution for unmarried mothers, and was now being supported by welfare while she went to a junior college. Her baby was about three months old when they moved in, and she told Mrs. Prince that a friend would take the baby while she was in school. Within a week, this arrangement, if it had existed at all, collapsed, and Dolores became quite ill with a gynecological problem. Mrs. Prince took care of her and the baby, took the mother to the hospital for treatment, and fixed meals for them both. Once back at school, Dolores continued to expect care from Mrs. Prince, who in fact found someone who would babysit for the young mother within the price allowed by welfare. Dolores stopped in constantly and told Mrs. Prince all her difficulties with boyfriends, showed her the expensive cosmetics she bought, and wangled invitations to join family meals when it became plain that she had not bought any food for herself and the baby. Mrs. Prince scolded Dolores as though she were one of her own teenagers but with as little effect.

Mrs. Prince: You know all I've been telling you about Dolores— well, it's minor to what happened today. I got up at about eight o'clock and I noticed Dolores' door in the back hallway had a note on it. And it said, "Molly, I have some tests today and the babysitter is sick, so please listen for Laurie and put her in the playpen when she wakes up. I'll be home soon." She didn't have the nerve to *ask* me! And she didn't come home till four o'clock and nothing to eat in the house for that baby and not even a clean diaper. And I'll bet she hadn't even gone to school!

Consultant: I wonder what could be done [for] Dolores so she could have some fun for her age and still take care of that baby?

Mrs. Prince: I've talked and talked and threatened to tell the welfare and then she cries and says she'd have to go back home and her mother doesn't want her and so I get soft— and it's all over again.

Consultant: I wonder if her caseworker knows how it is?

Mrs. Prince: Well, she's been here and I heard her scolding Dolores for skipping school, but I don't know if she knows about the rest—

Consultant: Dolores seems to talk pretty freely to everyone, so would you think it would be all right if you had a talk with the caseworker to see how to get things a little more settled down?

Mrs. Prince: No, I wouldn't want to get mixed up with that—

she's made her bed and she just has to lie in it—only I'm sorry for that baby.

Here, the consultant must determine the dynamics of the situation and the course of action to take. Perhaps, in this case, the consultant might assume responsibility for arranging a conference with the welfare worker. Mrs. Prince might be included or at least invited to attend. The consultant must weigh the possible outcomes of the intervention against the danger of damaging the self-confidence of the natural neighbor. Any implication that the natural neighbor is not competent to deal with the situation may cause her irrevocable withdrawal from that role. Professionalization of roles formerly carried out by natural systems has had that effect many times in the past. Natural networks are fragile and depend on the strength of the natural neighbor. The importance of dealing with them with great care cannot be overestimated.

When partnership efforts like those attempted by Mrs. Towne are successful, they not only benefit the child and the family but also strengthen the partnership bond between consultant and natural neighbor. If, as in Mrs. Prince's case, the effort fails and the family must be brought to official attention, there may still be a bond formed by joint effort and mutual disappointment. The consultant can help in either case by reviewing the action in terms of the experience itself and especially by emphasizing the positive role played by the natural neighbor, regardless of the outcome. Thus, a major objective of consultation may be achieved even when specific results are not achieved. In future instances, the natural neighbor will be more able to cope and more confident in intervening. An upward spiral of greater skill, better self-image, and more confidence to reach out is a likely and desirable consequence.

Some Conclusions

Unless maltreatment has been extremely severe, it is customary to have children returned to their parents from foster placement when the home situation has improved in the judgment of the court. Even if the reunited family is not always accessible—if, for instance, it has not remained in the neighborhood or has only recently moved into the natural neighbor's orbit—the interest and acceptance that the natural neighbor can offer may still considerably affect the treatment that the children will receive at home. The consultant can encourage the natural neighbor to reach out to the parents, to make an effort to integrate them as much as possible into the network, and to influence public opinion in their favor if possible.

Continuing Contact. The consultant will rarely need to encourage natural neighbors to maintain contact with families and children. This is true even after action has been taken that disrupts the family—action that may precipitate a new crisis by leading to increased isolation and shame. Natural neighbors are likely to continue their contact as a matter of course. They are not used to the professional approach of "closing a case," and it takes very little support to see to it that the matter remains "open." Here, the continuing interest and approval shown by the consultant can help the natural neighbor withstand criticism—criticism that is especially difficult to accept since the neighbor is more accustomed to gratitude and approval than to their opposites.

There is an important gain to the consultant in the opportunity to observe how services are seen from the viewpoint of recipients. The window that this opens into the ongoing, daily existence of network members provides a new perspective on the kind of services that might decrease recidivism. It may be possible for the consultant to influence the professional community, the parent agency and others, as a result of this firsthand view. For example, the consultant's success may encourage the agency to recommend the establishment of parent groups. Collaboration with the agency may be helpful in other ways as well. Without the consultation relationship, the agency may close the case when children are returned and the family is reestablished, leaving family members to fend for themselves.

Natural neighbors tend to feel that they are "not doing anything." For many, this modest disclaimer is really only a manner of speech since they are well aware of their activity and its effectiveness. For others, especially for people who have had jobs with well-defined duties and rewards, it may be an expression of dissatisfaction with the vague outlines of the role they have assumed. If the consultant is sensitive to expressions of this kind, to statements about envying the professional job role, and to wishes on the part of the natural neighbor that she might have trained for it, the consultant can and should point out in as many ways as possible the importance of the natural neighbor role and its unique power to affect the future of children and their families.

Record Keeping. Both the consultant and the natural neighbor should keep records from the very beginning of the relationship. At the time of recruitment, the consultant should explain to the natural neighbor that the consultation method is a new one and that, in order to describe it to others and to keep track of its development, some kind of record keeping is essential. The consultant should have in mind a simple system that will require the natural neighbor to do no more than record contacts (who was seen or spoken to about children or family affairs in general), taking some care not to put emphasis on keeping track only of maltreatment. Keeping records of what they do is a practice quite alien to natural neighbors. Typically, they will not carry it out in the systematic manner that professionals would like for use in their reports and research. Professionals will need to discipline themselves not to take a supervisory role in this matter. Rather, they should attempt to secure the information in ways that are not objectionable to the natural neighbor. In some instances, it has worked well to arrange for a monthly fact-gathering interview in which the professional brings a tape recorder and encourages the natural neighbor to tell her "what's been going on," even asking questions about someone previously mentioned but not discussed again. The consultant will need to explain more than once how this material will be used and how it will be kept confidential. A fact-gathering session is also sometimes an effective antidote to the natural neighbor's sense of "not doing anything." If the consultant can use the transcription and analyses of the taped material to produce some figures on the numbers of contacts the natural neighbor actually has had over the month and something about their outcomes, the sense of not doing anything may be replaced by a feeling of accomplishment.

Cultural Differences. Before they even begin their contacts with natural neighbors, consultants will have made attempts to familiarize themselves with the culture of the neighborhood in which they are working. But they are likely to find, as they come to know the culture from the "inside," that they are confronted with behavior that seems to them to be neglecting and abusing, although it is not perceived as such by the natural neighbors. Physical force applied to children is often the most upsetting manifestation of differences in values. "Spare the rod and spoil the child" is still a maxim in some groups. The natural neighbor may or may not subscribe to such ideas in the same way the parents do. In any event, it may be futile to accuse parents of abuse when they feel they are carrying out their parental responsibilities. Accusations may also serve to increase their alienation from the wider society and intensify abusive behavior as they assert their parental rights to deal with their children's wrongdoing in ways that they believe will solve the problem. If the consultant and the natural neighbor can support each other in such circumstances, the anger of the parents may be dampened. Moreover, their combined attempt to arrive at a solution to the problem will be less colored by their feelings than if each were working alone. If the natural neighbor does not share the parents' values, it might be well to seek out someone in the network who does and attempt to get such an individual to act as a go-between. Where there are natural healers, such as the *cuanderos* in Mexican and Mexican-American groups, the natural neighbor may find them a source of strength, even of intervention.

Cost Effectiveness. This chapter has presented a way in which those who are already in touch with their friends and neighbors as helpers can be strengthened and supported by a professional consultant. When the partnership between consultant and natural neighbor is well established, it can act as an anticipatory device to head off maltreatment, as well as an ongoing support for those who, for many reasons, cannot by themselves remain within the limits of healthy childcare.

Little has been said about the financial feasibility of such a plan because, ideally, child welfare policies should be determined not by financial considerations but by humane ones. But the hard fact remains that policies and programs are, and probably must be, determined by the availability of funds and public willingness to invest those funds. The public, in the case of child maltreatment, is most concerned with flagrant abuse and extreme neglect. It wants them stopped and the offenders punished. Funding prevention programs of any kind is never popular. But, happily, using consultants with natural neighbors does seem to be very economical when compared to asking professionals to carry the entire burden of preventing maltreatment. One professional can be in contact with at least fifteen natural neighbors at one time, and each natural neighbor, in turn, may have some contact with, and gain considerable knowledge of, perhaps seventy-five families in the course of a year. For both prevention and intervention, numbers like these are appealing.

In this chapter, the consultation model has been presented as one approach to the problem of child maltreatment. Although no single approach can provide all the answers to the difficult questions posed by child abuse and neglect, this model appears to be highly effective in many instances.

CHAPTER 8

Improving Formal Services for Mothers and Children

David L. Olds

Authors of previous chapters have urged a rethinking of the origin of child maltreatment, highlighting the role that social disintegration and family isolation play in such behavior. They have encouraged the use of informal social networks as a way to meet the problem. In light of the complex interrelations of psychiatric, sociological, and situational factors associated with maltreatment (Parke and Collmer, 1975), however, we should

Note: The work reported in this chapter is supported by a grant from the Bureau of Maternal and Child Health Research Grants Division (MC-R-360403-01), Department of Health, Education, and Welfare. The author wishes to thank Barbara Bauer, Jay Belsky, and James Lombardi for their helpful comments on an earlier version of this chapter and Robert Chamberlin, Jacqueline Roberts, and Robert Tatelbaum for helping to shape the material presented here.

be wary of concluding that strengthening social networks by itself will be sufficient to deal with this disturbing problem. The fact that social isolation is almost always present in cases of maltreatment does not necessarily mean that efforts to integrate isolated parents into informal social networks will prevent maltreatment. Other difficulties within the family may undermine the success of this approach. Isolated parents, for example, may differ from those belonging to close-knit networks in subtle psychological ways, such as being unwilling or unable to affiliate with family members, to make friends, or to participate in community organizations. Consequently, these individuals may resist programmatic pressures to interact with other family members, neighbors, or providers of formal services. A program emphasizing the enhancement of informal social networks without regard to other personal or family needs may then be insufficient to deal with the problem.

Since there appear to be at least as many factors contributing to maltreatment as there are different forms of abuse and neglect, it makes sense to remain flexible at this early stage of our attempt to deal with it. Strengthening informal social networks appears to be a valuable tactic, but it probably should be just one part of a comprehensive strategy addressing maltreatment rather than the sole approach. A wide range of formal as well as informal community resources is needed to respond to the stressful psychological, medical, and social conditions that undermine parents' abilities to provide appropriate care for their children. Moreover, since we know so little about the effectiveness of intervention, it is important to take a cautious, scientific approach to the development of new services. The fields of health and human services are filled with partisans who strongly advocate particular service strategies in the absence of satisfactory supportive evidence or even in the face of evidence contradicting their approach. While the problem of child maltreatment cannot wait for a definitive piece of research outlining the way to proceed, we should examine carefully what we are doing with children and families in this area. This becomes especially important now that funds for services are increasingly in jeopardy; without careful research and evaluation, we may waste scarce resources on ineffective programs.

The present chapter describes the Prenatal/Early Infancy Project (PEIP), a program of service and research designed to improve the childbearing success and childrearing competencies of first time mothers who have limited resources to manage the demands of pregnancy and early childcare. The services of the project were established, first, to help parents cope with the often unending chain of stressful events experienced during pregnancy and the first two years of the baby's life. By drawing on a comprehensive array of formal as well as informal community resources, the program attempts to prevent a wide range of health and developmental problems in children, including maltreatment. It should be emphasized that the prevention of maltreatment is an important, although only small, part of the work reported here. Second, as these services are being provided, a systematic effort is made to determine whether unfavorable environmental conditions for pregnancy and early childrearing have been improved and, if so, whether these improved conditions have indeed enhanced the health and development of the children whose families are enrolled in the project.

Background

The Prenatal/Early Infancy Project is operating in a rural county located in New York State's Appalachian region. The county has a population of approximately 100,000 and includes a small city with about 40,000 residents. There are indications that many families in the community are living under difficult circumstances. Not only were rates of reported and substantiated child abuse within the three years prior to the development of the program among the very highest in the state (New York State Department of Social Services, 1974, 1975, 1976; "Report of the Family Life Development Center," 1976), but during the period from 1971 to 1974 the rates of prematurity and infant mortality also were reported to be among the state's highest (*Vital Statistics of New York State,* 1975). Moreover, throughout this six-year period (1971 to 1977), unemployment rates hovered around 10 percent. Clearly, some additional family support services were needed to offset the stresses of unem-

ployment and to help create a better environment for pregnancy and early childrearing among high-risk families in this
community.

The present project grew out of a children's health and
developmental screening program known as Comprehensive
Interdisciplinary Developmental Services (CIDS). Originally
funded by the Appalachian Regional Commission, CIDS uses
the battery of Denver Developmental Screening Tests to identify young children in need of further evaluation and treatment.
When potential problems are identified, the parents are helped
to find needed services in the community. In an attempt to find
out whether some of the health and developmental problems
identified by CIDS might be prevented, I drafted the present
project and shared it with key representatives of the local health
and human services community. For more than a year and a
half, this committee met regularly to further refine the program
plan and make arrangements for service coordination. During
this period, funds were sought from a variety of federal, state,
and private agencies, and a collaborative arrangement was developed with the departments of obstetrics, gynecology, and
pediatrics at the University of Rochester Medical Center. In
March of 1977, a grant was awarded to CIDS by the Bureau of
Maternal and Child Health Research Grants Division (Department of Health, Education, and Welfare) to fund the first two
years of the six-year demonstration and research project. The
first year of the project was devoted to research and to program
development and included working with a set of pilot families
to further refine research and program methodologies.

As part of the preliminary work involved in developing
this project, my colleagues at the University of Rochester
(Robert Chamberlin and Robert Tatelbaum) and I carried out a
review of the literature concerning problems with pregnancy,
infant health, and social, emotional, and intellectual functioning
(Olds and others, 1978). We concluded that a number of difficulties experienced by mothers and children in each of these
areas might be prevented by improving the delivery of preventive services during pregnancy and infancy. We identified
two problems with the current system of formal care that
seemed particularly important. First, families most needing pre-

ventive health services are least likely to take advantage of them. For a variety of reasons, pregnant mothers at greatest risk for pregnancy complications and for problems coping with their children use traditional health and human services least. Second, even if a mother and her baby are seen in a doctor's office, clinic, or welfare office, the practitioner is often unaware of the degree to which different difficulties facing the family interact to undermine individual health, family functioning, and parents' attempts to care for their child.

As a result of these findings, we concluded that a key feature of any attempt to improve the delivery of preventive services would be a strong outreach component, including frequent home visits. Since many of the issues with which we were concerned touched on issues of maternal and child health, we decided that registered nurses would be the best candidates to carry out the home-visitation activities. Because of the complex interrelation of adverse factors in the prenatal and infancy environments, the nurses were assigned three basic responsibilities —to educate parents concerning the myriad influences on fetal and infant development, to create informal support among family members and friends to encourage parents to improve their health practices and parenting behavior, and to link parents with other needed health and human services in the community. This kind of strategy, we believe, creates a basis for flexibly and effectively responding to a wide range of family needs, some of which place the child at risk for maltreatment. In addition to home visitation by nurses, transportation for prenatal and well-child care is provided to help families gain access to traditional medical services. Finally, all children are screened for health and developmental problems at one and two years of age so that serious problems can be identified and treated at early stages.

The overall strategy is based on two complementary concepts—timing and ecology. We believe that the *timing* of the intervention is crucial. Gordon (1971), for example, provided evidence that the earlier work is begun with parents, the more effective it is. PEIP services are begun during the prenatal period for two reasons. First, there is ample evidence to suggest that events taking place during pregnancy can have enduring effects on the functioning of the organism (Abramowicz and Kass, 1966; Sameroff and Chandler, 1975; Weiner and others, 1968). Second, it has been our practical experience that offering assistance once the baby is born (possibly after a problem has emerged) is often interpreted by parents as a message that they have cared for their child poorly. If assistance is offered before the birth of the first child, when all families have questions and special needs, parents are less defensive.

The emphasis on comprehensive services grows out of a theoretical framework known as human *ecology* (Bronfenbrenner, 1977; Brim, 1975). According to this view, a variety of factors operating within the family and community determine opportunities for the child's growth and development. In the present program, three major influences on the well-being of the child have been identified as focuses of intervention: the child's parents, other family members and friends, and additional health and human services in the community (see Figure 1). By carrying out his or her work at different "levels" of the ecological system (with parents, with the parents' informal support system, and with the larger health and human services community) the nurse is in a powerful position to create a salutary environment for healthy development. As we reviewed the literature, we were surprised to find that virtually no one had carried out satisfactory research on the effectiveness of comprehensive preventive services. Our commitment to rigorous evaluation became even more important in light of this scarcity of information about the effectiveness of this approach for high-risk families. A systematic research design is thus an integral part of the program. In order to determine how effective each major component of this strategy is, families are randomly assigned to receive different subsets of the total intervention, and these groups are then compared in terms of the quality of the prenatal and infancy environment and the health and development of the children.

PEIP Services

The PEIP services are directed toward families in which mothers bearing first children are *either* teenagers, single, or

Figure 1. Focuses of Intervention in the Prenatal/Early Infancy Project

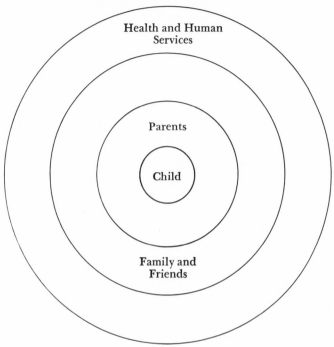

poor. In order to participate, mothers must enroll sometime before the twenty-fourth week of pregnancy; we insist on early
enrollment to allow sufficient time for our services to affect the
health of the mother. We chose to serve those groups of mothers who are at risk for pregnancy complications and parenting
dysfunctions (Abramowicz and Kass, 1966; Sameroff and
Chandler, 1975). We decided to work with firstborns because of
our belief that the skills parents develop with first children will
carry over to their care of later children, thus maximizing the
impact of the intervention. Even though the services are concen-
trated on these high-risk families, any mother bearing a first
child is welcomed into the project. By following this procedure,
we are able to avoid stigmatizing the program as being available
only for the poor or only for people with problems.

A question frequently asked about our program is how
families meeting the enrollment criteria are found. Fortunately,

more than 90 percent of the families meeting the criteria outlined above seek prenatal care sometime prior to their seventh
month of pregnancy. Consequently, most of our recruitment
takes place in a local health department prenatal clinic and
through the offices of private obstetricians. Referral procedures
also have been established with the local schools and Planned
Parenthood clinic. (Significantly, as the program has grown, an
increasingly large number of referrals have come from young
mothers already enrolled in the project.) Although families sent
to us by these agencies do not always meet the program criteria,
they nevertheless are enrolled if they choose to participate. This
procedure allows the program to maintain its objective of being
available to all families having a first child, while simultaneously
allowing it to focus services on those families most in need. At
present, more than 85 percent of the qualifying families who
learn about the services and research participate in the project.
We expect 350 to 400 families to enroll in the project over the
course of its first two years as a result of our recruitment efforts. The following sections detail the services available to the
families who enroll in the project. As noted above, because of
the need to determine program effectiveness, families are randomly assigned to receive different subsets of these services.

While visiting families every other week for approximately one and one-half hours, the nurses are engaged in three
activities designed to enhance the conditions for bearing and
rearing children. First, and most important, they function as
home-based educators providing parents with emotional support, information, and guidance about factors that affect fetal
development, the birth, and the well-being of the child. Second,
in order to extend and intensify their work with the mother,
the nurses encourage the assistance of friends and other family
members (especially the father, when present) in the pregnancy,
birth experience, and early care of the infant. Third, while providing the home-based education program, the nurses often
notice that parents are preoccupied with survival problems
(such as marital conflicts and difficulties with finances and
housing) that prevent them from translating their knowledge
about good health practices and childcare into effective action.

Consequently, the nurses link these families with additional health and human services so that these pressing problems can begin to be resolved.

Home-Based Education. One of the most important objectives of the home-based education program is to provide emotional support to mother and family. Examples of supportive nursing behavior include responding to parents' concerns, helping them clarify their feelings, praising areas that parents are handling well, being available to parents in times of stress, and encouraging them to develop their own problem-solving skills. To be truly supportive, it is essential that nurses respect parents' values and not try to impose their own.

The PEIP home visitor is trained to help the family understand and deal with the following eight general issues: prenatal and infancy nutritional requirements; fetal development and factors that may compromise the development of the unborn child (for example, smoking, drinking, or the use of drugs by the mother); complications of pregnancy; labor and delivery; early care of the newborn, including the importance of postpartum parent-newborn interaction; the infant as an individual with his or her own special characteristics; basic principles of infant health and safety; and activities in which parents can engage their babies that will enhance the infants' social, emotional, and intellectual development. Special attention is focused on helping parents select and use a method of birth control. Parents are encouraged to space their children appropriately so that the mother can recuperate from the first pregnancy and both parents can devote more attention to the firstborn. Underlying all these activities is our objective of enhancing the health and development of the child by improving his or her physical environment and the qualities of parent-infant attachment.

Many of these topics have implications concerning the extent to which the family is at risk for maltreatment. During the mother's pregnancy, for example, the nurse may develop an impression that parents may later have difficulties in providing appropriate care for their children. While visiting in the home, the nurse considers various family situations in light of the causes of abuse and neglect identified by psychiatric, sociological, and social-situational models of maltreatment (Parke and Collmer, 1975). Of special importance are the following questions:

• Does either parent report having experienced a difficult or violent childhood?
• Do the parents have realistic expectations about the baby and the demands of childcare?
• Does either parent appear to have any emotional difficulties, especially poor impulse control?
• Are there any factors in the home that may create later stresses for parents and undermine their control of impulses (for example, unemployment, overcrowded housing, marital problems)?
• Do the parents appear to be isolated from sources of support such as family, friends, or neighbors?

This last question is of special importance, since Garbarino (1977a) and others have shown that the isolated parent is particularly given to child maltreatment. Information on these topics is used by the nurses to plan future home visits and to develop ways to employ community resources in aiding the family.

Recent research suggests that interaction between parents and infants soon after delivery contributes to the development of an affectional bond between them (Klaus and Kennell, 1976). As a result of this accumulating body of evidence, the home-visitation nurses encourage parents to take full advantage of any opportunities for interacting with the newborn infant during the immediate postpartum period. The absence of early parental involvement has been suggested as a factor contributing to the high rates of maltreatment among premature infants, who typically are rushed to neonatal intensive care units before their parents have an opportunity to interact with them (Parke and Collmer, 1975; Klaus and Kennell, 1976). Nurses thus work with parents in the home to promote the following specific parental behaviors in the hospital: minimal use of medications

during labor and delivery so mother and baby are alert after-
wards; opportunities for both parents to hold and for the
mother to nurse the infant for an hour or longer after birth;
rooming-in with the baby during the hospital stay so mother
and newborn can become acquainted within a supportive, structured environment; and, for newborns in intensive care, visiting
and feeding by the parents as frequently as possible.

Toward the end of pregnancy, the nurses help parents
prepare for birth and early childcare in the home. During this
time, efforts are made to assist the mother and father to develop realistic expectations about the infant, especially with
respect to the demands it will place upon them. Once the baby
is born, emphasis is placed on helping parents develop a finely
attuned responsiveness to their child as a basis for healthy
parent-child communication. Toward this end, the PEIP nurse
visits mother and newborn within the first few days after they
have returned home from the hospital to make sure they are
well and also to administer the Brazelton Neonatal Assessment
Scale (Brazelton, 1973). In this way she can enhance the parents' understanding of the unique characteristics and abilities of
the infant. For example, does the baby "cuddle" when held,
soothe easily, or adapt readily to changes in its environment? In
an attempt to help parents accommodate their care to the specific needs of their infant, the nurse uses this information to
encourage parents to think about ways their baby is likely to
respond to its environment during the following few weeks.

At this time, another piece of information relevant to the
issue of maltreatment is gathered. Since it is known that a first
child tends to disturb the equilibrium of the family and create
stress by requiring that parents assume new roles (Bakan, 1971),
babies who are "difficult" (irritable, not easily soothed, "un-
cuddly," and so forth), create additional stresses for parents
that may lead to abuse or neglect. In addition, passivity or
lethargy on the part of an infant may also place it at risk for
maltreatment because the baby's inability to send clear signals
may interfere with the development of mother-infant attachment (Parke and Collmer, 1975).

Beginning in the first few days after the child's birth and

continuing throughout its first two years of life, the nurses talk with parents about the normal course of infant development as part of their attempt to help parents develop realistic expectations for the child. In order to assist parents to better appreciate the abilities of their babies, the PEIP nurses have been taught to use the Denver Developmental Screening Tests, which help them assess the babies in terms of language, personal-social functioning, and fine and gross motor functioning. The Denver test is also useful for discovering developmental delays. Any potential problems that are uncovered can be evaluated more thoroughly by a pediatrician and treated before they become more serious.

The early care of the first child provides unique opportunities for the nurse to discuss with parents things they can do with their infant to make their own lives less difficult, while creating opportunities for the infant's growth and learning. Most important, the nurse can:

- Encourage parents to respond sensitively to the sometimes subtle signals and cues infants use to demonstrate their needs.
- Teach parents games and activities that they can play with their baby to stimulate cognitive and motor development.
- Stress how important it is that parents talk with their baby to facilitate language development.
- Help parents organize their household so that the infant has opportunities to explore and learn, while its safety and that of the household are preserved.
- Teach parents whose infants will soon be toddlers how to provide positive reinforcement when dealing with such practical disciplinary problems as toilet training, feeding difficulties, and bedtime resistance.

Because the nurses are themselves parents, they have first-hand experience to share with mothers in the program. While working with parents, the nurses reassure them that frustrations associated with being a parent are not unusual and that feeling temporary anger is common when caring for children.

Special report forms have been prepared to assist the

nurses in making systematic evaluations of family functioning in each of the areas cited above. Rather than following a regimented teaching schedule, however, the nurses generally try to let parents set the pace and tenor of the home visits. Topics discussed first are those about which parents are most interested or concerned. Nevertheless the nurses do see to it that all topics are uniformly covered with parents within designated time periods. For each of these topics, detailed protocols have been written to help guide the nurses in their resolution of problems in particular areas. These protocols are currently being revised and elaborated on the basis of our experience in the field; they eventually will be turned into manuals so that the program can be carried out in other areas if we are successful in meeting our present objectives.

In general, parents' confidence and skill in caring for their babies can best be improved by praising and encouraging them in activities that they do well. Moreover, throughout all the home-visit activities, the nurse encourages independent thinking and action on the part of parents. To increase their independence and self-confidence, we have established a lending library of books and materials on all aspects of pregnancy and early childcare for interested parents. Many of the materials are written for individuals with only rudimentary reading skills. We also provide all parents with a set of educational pamphlets and a personal copy of an easy-to-read book entitled *Child Care* (St. Geme, 1978) that they can use as a reference when confronted with common health or behavioral problems. We have been happily surprised to find that parents are reading more of the materials than we had anticipated.

Assistance of Family and Friends. The home-visitation program is oriented toward the inclusion of friends and other family members. Although 65 percent of our young mothers are unmarried, a large number of them are living with the father of the child or have boyfriends who live in the community. In addition to having fathers nearby, mothers in PEIP often live either in extended family situations or with friends. Regardless of the exact living arrangements, these "significant others" are encouraged to sit in on the nurse's home visits if the mother so desires. We believe that this kind of emotional support for the mother can assist her in coping with pregnancy, labor, delivery, and early childrearing. Special emphasis is placed on involving the father. While other intervention programs have failed to get fathers involved (White and others, 1972), we have tried to avoid the pitfalls of these programs by scheduling home visits at times when fathers can participate and by considering fathers' special needs as parents. In the case of working fathers, this means that nurses must pay evening and weekend visits. During these visits, fathers are encouraged to attend childbirth education classes, to help mothers improve their diets and cut down on smoking, drinking, and use of drugs, to be present for labor and delivery, and to interact with mother and baby during the immediate postpartum period. Once mother and baby have returned home, fathers are encouraged to help with household tasks and to take an active role in caring for and playing with the child. These procedures are expected to create in fathers a greater sense of purpose and responsibility for their families.

Where fathers are not present, the mother is encouraged to select a support figure, usually a friend or her own mother, who is available to help her. And, where possible, other family members and friends are urged to support the goals of the program. One example of network members who supported better maternal health practices involved a mother in the pilot study who was having a hard time controlling her excessive weight gain. Our nurse's advice to replace cookies and Coke with nutritional snacks went unheeded until the woman's younger sister was asked to remind the mother of the nurse's advice. Another young woman found it difficult to cut down on smoking until the nurse enlisted the help of the young woman's friends to remind her of the harmful effect of smoking on the fetus. Unfortunately, the involvement of other family members is sometimes limited by institutional barriers. At one of the local hospitals, for instance, only the husband is allowed to enter the delivery room with the mother.

Even when fathers are present, mothers are encouraged toward the end of pregnancy to identify friends or relatives who might provide additional support to them if they have temperamentally difficult babies. Having a reliable, trustworthy friend or relative to help with an irritable or colicky baby or to provide periodic relief from the demands of full-time parenting is considered especially important in relieving parental stresses that might lead to child maltreatment. It should be noted, nonetheless, that not all informal social networks serve constructive functions for the child and family. One young pregnant woman in our pilot study, who as a young child had been practically tortured for bed-wetting, was living at home in a large extended family in which members commonly disciplined their children by slapping them, often on the face. In spite of this young woman's integration into a social network, the norms and feedback of network members with respect to childrearing actually contributed to maltreatment. The nurse's task in such cases is then complicated by the need to counteract these adverse influences. In this particular case, however, we were able to arrange for the young woman and her newborn child to spend several weeks after delivery with a stable neighbor whom the mother thought of as a grandmother. Once mother and baby were functioning adequately together they moved into an apartment on their own. The neighbor continues to serve as a "lifeline" source of support for this young woman in times of crisis.

Our approach to the facilitation of informal network ties presumes the presence of at least some effective connections with network members. Our experience in the pilot study, however, has challenged this working assumption. In at least two cases, young single mothers were totally isolated from friends, neighbors, and relatives in spite of efforts by their nurse home-visitor and several other formal service providers to establish effective communication. In both cases, situational factors and histories of traumatic upbringing seemed to contribute to emotional dysfunctions that inhibited these parents' ability to reach out and trust others or to allow others to understand them. These two mothers were walled in by the barrriers discussed by Benjamin Gottlieb in Chapter Three. In one of the cases, a sixteen-year-old pregnant girl had been sexually molested by a relative over the course of several years before being removed from her home. Eventually she was placed in a group home with ten delinquent children, since there were no foster care homes available. Working with this young woman, our nurse soon became quite discouraged because of the girl's isolation from any network of friends, neighbors, or relatives. At the time of this writing, our nurse was trying to convince the department of social services to place this young woman in a foster care home where both she and her newborn would be provided with an extended family environment. In this case the girl was deprived of *both* informal and formal sources of support.

The second case involved a young woman who was once a member of a local gang that was involved in the sale and use of drugs. Upon her release from a girls' reformatory where she had been sent for trafficking in heroin, she broke all ties with members of the gang and moved in with her father and younger brother. During pregnancy, she refused to go outside her home for fear of being ridiculed as "fat" and "ugly." In addition to providing the home-based education services described above, our nurse arranged for another young mother from a YWCA program to visit this young woman in her home and to encourage her to meet other mothers participating in the YWCA program.

Thus, we seek to facilitate informal network ties by reinforcing existing connections with friends, neighbors, and relatives. When such ties are absent, we seek other, more formal sources of support to reinforce parents' childbearing and childrearing efforts. In our approach to the use of informal social networks, nurses work *through the family* to identify sources of support, whereas in the approach outlined by Diane Pancoast and Alice Collins (see Chapters Six and Seven), the network *itself,* specifically central figures, is the focus of intervention. We see the use of formal social services as a useful supplement to informal social networks, especially when informal supports are weak.

Linkages with Other Health and Human Services. The third major activity of the PEIP home visitor is to help families find and use other health and human services in the community. All parents are routinely encouraged to enroll in childbirth education classes, to keep prenatal and well-child care appointments, and to make use of formal classes designed to teach effective childcare. In addition, families are referred to specific social services when these are needed to help them resolve particular problems that disrupt their lives.

Families enrolled in PEIP receive their prenatal and well-child care either at private physicians' offices or at the local health department clinic, which is free to all families in the community. In order to strengthen the delivery of health care from these settings, the PEIP nurses send regular written reports containing information gathered during visits (nutritional inadequacies, health hazards, emotional or social disturbances, and so forth) that may help physicians and nurses provide more informed and sensitive care in the office. As necessary, office visits are arranged to discuss problem cases. During these visits, the physician and nursing staff explain to the PEIP home visitor their medical care plan. With this information, the home visitor clarifies for the patient the physician's recommendations and thereby reinforces his or her advice. We think that these nurse-mediated linkages between patient's home and physician's office will result in better health care because doctors' directives will be more consistently followed. As an illustration, one young woman in the pilot study reported a lifelong habit of eating unusual substances. She had not revealed this to professionals other than her PEIP nurse because she felt guilty about this practice. After the nurse discussed this issue with the young woman's obstetrician, prenatal vitamins with iron were prescribed. This, along with dietary advice, eliminated the problem.

Since the PEIP nurses have completed local childbirth education classes as part of their training, they are in a good position to encourage parents to do the same. In childbirth education classes, parents are exposed to a systematic educational program for pregnancy, birth, and early childcare (which they can then discuss with the PEIP nurse in their home). It is perhaps even more important that at the classes parents meet others with whom they can share common interests and concerns. It is expected that additional support for the young family will grow out of this experience. Since the implementation of our program, the attendance of young, single, and poor parents at childbirth education classes has risen demonstrably. Before PEIP was established, childbirth education classes were attended almost exclusively by middle-class married couples. One problem has been arranging transportation for some prospective parents to and from the classes, since the transportation provided in the program is only for regularly scheduled visits to the physician for prenatal and well-child care. But arrangements have been made with church groups and other members of the class who own cars to provide transportation.

There are two ongoing classes in the community established to help parents learn effective methods of caring for their children: one of the local hospitals offers a special class in infancy, which is usually attended by middle-class parents, and the YWCA offers a young mothers' program (primarily for teenagers) that combines recreational activities for mothers, child-care services, and information on parenting. PEIP nurses encourage mothers to attend one of these groups, so that they will have the opportunity of learning more about their babies and meeting other parents with whom they may become friends. By learning appropriate expectations for infant development and overcoming isolation, parents will be better prepared to respond appropriately to their babies' changing developmental needs.

As noted above, many of the families enrolled in PEIP are preoccupied with pressing problems, such as marital difficulties, unemployment, unsafe or crowded housing, and financial or emotional difficulties. Recognizing that such problems undermine the effects of their educational efforts and create special problems for the parents' care of the infants, the nurses help their families find and use appropriate services in the community. A number of the parents in the program have been referred to help with job training programs; continuing their high school education; finding infant daycare; mental health counseling; marital counseling; legal matters; diet planning and budgeting; diet supplementation from the Women, Infants, and Children (WIC) program; obtaining food stamps, Medicaid and public assistance; selecting methods of birth control from their physician or Planned Parenthood clinic; and deciding whether to surrender their baby for adoption.

Helping families find solutions to pressing personal problems is one of the many ways the PEIP nurses relieve some of the stress that often creates a background for child abuse or neglect. Furthermore, we believe that, with these stresses reduced, parents eventually will be able to devote more time and energy to enjoying life with their baby. For instance, two of the mothers in our pilot study who themselves had been mistreated as children displayed such inadequate emotional functioning, including poor impulse control and low self-esteem, that their nurse felt they needed professional attention. The nurse suggested mental health counseling, a suggestion that the families accepted surprisingly well. One of the young mothers requested that her nurse attend the first session with her. Her nurse agreed but explained that she would go only the first time. After counseling began, the nurse reported an improvement in communication between herself and the mother. Of course, we have no way of knowing whether counseling itself improved the mother's communication skills, but this experience is promising. Irrespective of its source, improved emotional stability obviously will enhance a parent's ability to learn from the home visitor and to function as a responsible provider of care to his or her children.

In order to ensure the effective use of community services, the PEIP nurses have met with the staff of all the major agencies with which they work and have identified key individuals within these agencies whom parents can call for help. These procedures were designed to facilitate the use of community services by personalizing the bureaucracy. The coordination of health and human services has been aided by the creation of a local steering committee that has guided the development of the service program since its inception.

A number of investigators have linked the absence of prenatal and well-child health services to a variety of health and developmental problems. Since many families enrolled in our project live in isolated rural regions of the county, we have provided families with a transportation backup system. In this way mother and child can be assisted in receiving regular prenatal and well-child medical care. In addition, health and developmental screening services are provided to all children at one and two years of age so that children with serious health and developmental problems in all service groups (described below) can be identified and treated. This helps us meet our ethical obligation to all families in the study. But the importance of providing health and developmental screening to all children will become even clearer as we consider the ethical issues involved in carrying out research for the program.

Overview of the Evaluation

In carrying out the evaluation of the program, participating families are randomly assigned into four service groups (outlined in Table 1), three of which represent subsets of the total

Table 1. Services Provided in Four Conditions

| | Service Conditions | | | |
	I	II	III	IV
Prenatal Period	a. Nurse home-visitation	a. Nurse home-visitation		
	b. Transportation	b. Transportation	b. Transportation	
Birth	— — — — —	— — — — —	— — — — —	— — — —
Infancy (birth to two years)	a. Nurse home-visitation			
	b. Transportation	b. Transportation	b. Transportation	
	c. Early and periodic screening	c. Early and periodic screening	c. Early and periodic screening	c. Early and periodic screening

intervention. By comparing the health and development of mothers and children receiving these different forms of help, we can determine the relative effectiveness of the services. Thus, in Service I, families receive the total intervention: (1) a nurse who visits them during the pregnancy and the first two years of the baby's life, (2) transportation for prenatal and well-child care, and (3) health and developmental screening for the infant at twelve and twenty-four months of age.

Since a number of programs provide services only during pregnancy, at considerably less cost than follow-up during infancy (and with perhaps as much impact on the child), it was reasoned that the value of prenatal home visitation by itself should be determined. The likelihood of the prenatal program having an impact is enhanced by the fact that nurses teach parents to request rooming-in and to ask to hold and explore their babies immediately after delivery (see Klaus and Kennell, 1976). Moreover, by comparing prenatal intervention with intervention that begins during pregnancy and continues into infancy, we can determine the value of continuity and infant follow-up. Hence, Service II is identical to Service I, except that the nurse visits the family only during pregnancy.

Much of the literature on prematurity and infant morbidity stresses the importance of regular medical care in preventing poor pregnancy outcomes and infant morbidity (Joint Commission on the Mental Health of Children, 1973). As a result of this emphasis on medical care, a number of programs, such as New York State's Child Health Assurance Program (New York's version of the Early Periodic Screening, Diagnosis and Treatment [EPSDT] program) provide medically related transportation services for Medicaid children. The value of this service in terms of child health and development, however, remains untested. For this reason, families in Service III are provided transportation for prenatal and well-child care, infant screening at twelve and twenty-four months, but no nurse.

The fourth group is provided infant screening at twelve and twenty-four months. Other than these screening services (which are presently available on request to all children in the community free of charge), the families in this condition are provided no other services by our program. Parents can, however, seek help from any other health and human services organizations in the community if they wish. By including Service IV we shall be able to determine whether PEIP services are of help beyond that which is already available in the community. The primary function of providing screening is to encourage parental participation in the program and allow us a means of meeting our ethical responsibility to detect serious health and developmental problems in the children. Families in all four treatment groups are followed from pregnancy through the infant's second year.

Random Assignment. All parents who enroll in the project agree to participate *before* they know which services they will receive. They understand that random assignment is necessary to make the groups of families receiving the different services as equal as possible before services are provided. While parents themselves almost never object to being randomly assigned, school nurses, social workers, and other persons responsible for the welfare of children and families who refer young mothers to us are more reluctant to accept random assignment. They sometimes refer families who, in their opinion, need a particular service, such as home visitation or transportation, and are disappointed when we explain that we cannot promise them any one set of services. In responding to their concern, we explain that, since there is no scientifically valid basis for knowing whether a particular service will be effective, it is important that studies with randomly assigned control groups be conducted. Only in this way will we know for certain whether it is worthwhile to provide any of these services. In the long run, evidence demonstrating service effectiveness should convince policy makers to budget more money for these services on a statewide and national basis. By carrying out a rigorously controlled evaluation of the program now, we may benefit a larger number of people in the future.

Practitioners usually are reassured when they realize that we have taken extensive steps to protect the welfare of all participants, including those families who have not received the nurse. That is, in the course of carrying out the project evaluation, we refer any child found to have a serious health or developmental problem in any service group to a pediatrician for evaluation and treatment. Any case of suspected child abuse or neglect is referred immediately to the department of social services, and any serious emotional or social problem on the part of parents (potential suicide or wife abuse, for example) is referred to an appropriate agency in the community. Our long-term commitment to scientifically valid research is thus tempered by our immediate ethical responsibilities and concern for all families with whom we are working.

Variables Analyzed. To evaluate the operation of the program, we assess three distinct sets of variables. First, we assess the *dependent variables* or outcomes of our research, that is, those aspects of the health and development of the child that we hope to improve through the prenatal and infancy interventions: birth outcomes, infant health indicators, and aspects of the infant's psychosocial development. Next we consider *intervening variables,* which include critical features of the prenatal and infancy environments that we are trying to ameliorate: mother's health, parenting behavior, the support of family and friends, family stresses and parents' use of community services. These variables are more directly influenced by the program than the dependent variables and are analyzed to determine (1) whether the services have had a significant impact upon those aspects of the prenatal and postnatal environment that they were designed to affect and (2) which aspects of the improved childbearing and childrearing environments contribute to improvements in child health and development. Finally, a set of *control variables* is assessed to determine the functioning of the mothers and their families before any services have been provided. These variables consist of aspects of the mother's own health, personality, and social situation. They were selected because of their possible influence on the family's ability to benefit from the services and their possible direct influence (independently of the program) on the health and development of the child. Their inclusion in the research allows us to make less biased estimates of program effects and to determine under which conditions the program is more and less successful.

From Science to Social Policy. Whenever a new social enterprise is undertaken, the cost of the endeavor must eventually be justified in terms of its social and financial benefits. With the exception of a follow-up of children reared in Iowa institutions (Skeels, 1966) and an evaluation of a rural health outreach program (D. Cowen and others, 1978), there exist few demonstrations of the cost effectiveness of providing early preventive services. This is especially unfortunate since experience has shown that whenever local, state, and federal budgets are cut, services for children and families are frequently the first to be eliminated. In view of these harsh realities, our research includes a cost-benefit analysis designed to compare the costs of the four sets of services and to weigh them against the social and financial benefits derived, such as reduced hospitalization in neonatal intensive care units, fewer payments for special services for the handicapped, and lowered Medicaid costs. Also examined are the families' reliance on the welfare system and parents' enrollment in job training and education programs. Since each of the treatment groups contains elements of existing state and federal programs aimed at helping disadvantaged families during pregnancy and early childhood (for example, the Maternal and Infancy Care Projects and the EPSDT program), the results of the foregoing analyses should contribute to the design of more effective services within these state and federal programs.

In recent years we have witnessed an increase in the number of teenage parents and young single women bearing children. One result of this trend has been an increase in the number of youngsters growing up in stressful, high-risk situations. These indicators make clear the need for stronger family planning efforts. Among those families where high-risk pregnancies are not prevented, however, other interventions are required to help parents cope with the inevitable tensions of bearing and rearing children on limited resources. The present investigation represents a preliminary attempt to address this serious national problem.

At this early stage in the research, we do not know to what degree the services provided by the project will prevent the myriad problems that afflict children growing up in abusive or neglecting families. Although we have devoted considerable effort to designing the nurse home-visitation program, we have established only a limited, cautious allegiance to this particular strategy. We are optimistic about the program, but we have no interest in promoting this approach if it proves to be ineffective. Our more basic allegiance is to preventing health and developmental difficulties among children born under high-risk circumstances. If the strategy outlined here is not as effective as we expect it to be, the investigation is designed to help us understand why it failed. At the same time, if the strategy proves to be effective, the research design will enable us to begin understanding what it is about the program that makes it successful. In either case, results of the project will contribute to more informed investigations and more effective services in the future.

Epilogue

James Garbarino
S. Holly Stocking

In the forgoing pages, we have explored personal social networks in some depth, presenting the rationale for involving them in prevention and treatment efforts, highlighting some of the issues professionals must face when they adopt a "social network" approach, and outlining a few ways to go about finding and using such networks.

In Chapter One, we tried to set the stage by noting the social context of child maltreatment and the need for strategies of treatment and prevention that would address this context. In the following chapter, Anne Tietjen put the matter of strategies in her own context, describing how human services work in another society where there is a comprehensive national family policy underlying an extensive network of family support systems. She reminded us that, while the issues before us are practical matters, our actions can be enhanced by a richer understanding of their cultural, empirical, and theoretical foundations.

In their chapters, Benjamin Gottlieb and Donald Warren

brought a fine-grained analysis to social networks—Gottlieb describing how personal social networks can and do work for parents, and Warren presenting what we know about *neighborhoods* as sources of and vehicles for helping. James Garbarino and Deborah Sherman followed up by proposing some practical strategies for assessing the neighborhood context of child maltreatment. And Diane Pancoast and Alice Collins described a consultation model they have used to harness natural helping networks to deal with child maltreatment. Pancoast discussed preparations for the consultation relationship, including the selection of neighborhoods on which to focus, while Collins described the dynamics of that relationship.

Finally, David Olds described one effort to coordinate formal and informal support systems to prevent a wide range of health and developmental problems in children, including maltreatment. His discussion highlighted the need for agency sensitivity to personal support systems and for systematic evaluation of interventions, whether they are consultation approaches or other forms of service delivery.

Numerous conclusions *might* be drawn from these discussions, but we think some of the most important are these:

Child maltreatment is a problem of environments as well as of individuals. It is a problem that often exists within families that are socially isolated—families without friends, relatives, or neighbors who can offer a variety of prosocial supports. And it is a problem we believe can be ameliorated if human services practitioners and public policy makers will but recognize, collaborate with, strengthen, and even create positive social networks.

Efforts to positively influence the social connections of families require indepth understanding of both families and their environments. Some neighborhoods and communities excel in personal social supports, others do not. Some individual families have access to certain kinds of help, but not to others. Professionals and policy makers who wish to influence the personal social networks of families need to immerse themselves in the individual and social "ecologies" of families.

Efforts to use personal social networks to treat and pre-

vent child maltreatment require a shift in professional perspective—from care*giver* and policy *maker* to *participant* in caregiving and policy making. Such efforts call for "empowering" others, for collaborating with nonprofessionals, and for relinquishing some of the red-taped "controls" that have traditionally bound bureaucracies to people and replacing them with bonds of human understanding. Such strategies will also help deal with the problem of "cultural differences" by promoting a more sensitive understanding of them.

Efforts to empower personal social networks on behalf of families should not be undertaken to the exclusion of more traditional "individualistic" efforts. No one approach is likely to solve the problem of child maltreatment. Like most social problems, it is multiply determined, and it demands multiple solutions.

Similarly, personal social networks should not be developed at the expense of more formal support systems. As Anne Tietjen and David Olds pointed out, no one support system can adequately perform without help from other systems. Our approaches need to reflect diversity, not single-minded enthusiasms.

Finally, approaches to social interventions, however promising they appear on the surface, need to be tested. Olds underlined this point in his chapter, and we further underline it here. Much practice and public policy are based, not on what we know, but on what we believe. Belief is powerful, but if we are to rationally plan our society, we need to *know* what works, and what does not, and why.

For professionals who are persuaded of the need to take a "social network" approach to child maltreatment, we offer these additional parting suggestions:

Communicate with the decision makers. As Diane Pancoast and Alice Collins pointed out, a decision to embark on the consultation model (or related strategies) means a major commitment of time and energy, at least initially. It should not be made lightly or without institutional support. Someone at or near the top of an agency or government organization should be involved in any decision to proceed with efforts to increase the protective behaviors in the environment of families.

Investigate existing resources. Despite a plethora of workshops and resource files in the human services, we constantly find ourselves "reinventing the wheel." Before launching a major effort to support and build upon the helping networks of families, find out what is already going on that may serve the purposes of increasing personal social resources for families. Are there neighborhood associations with an interest in natural neighbors? Are there PTAs that encourage parents to meet informally? Is there a pediatrician who holds meetings for prospective parents on a neighborhood basis? Are there existing programs that can be woven together?

Determine the most logical focal point for the project. No particular kind of agency or group will necessarily prove to be the best rallying point in every community. In some areas, the public child protective service office will be the logical agency around which to organize a program for increasing the protective resources of families. In other areas, the Family Service Association will be the best candidate. In still others, the focal point could be a group such as the Visiting Nurse Association. As we have tried to show in this book, the most cost-effective method for serving families and protecting children will be the method that builds upon existing resources and relationships. That method will no doubt vary from family to family, from community to community, and from neighborhood to neighborhood. One of the great traps is to assume that a certain set of principles or rules can be applied in all situations. This is not true in childrearing, and it is not true in "network rearing." Within limits, each child is different. Each has a temperament that must be considered when calculating the most effective parenting techniques. Likewise, each family and each neighborhood have a character, and one must appreciate that character if one is to be an effective consultant or community planner.

Become part of a network of helpers. Experience demonstrates that practitioners and decision makers cannot do it alone. An important part of the task before anyone who is trying to build protective resources for families is to become "well connected." Share this book with others who may be responsive to its ideas. Meet informally with colleagues. Contact others who share your interest in building positive social networks for families.

As we conclude this volume, we are reminded that in 1978, at the Third Annual National Conference on Child Abuse and Neglect, the first Henry Kempe Award for the best paper on child abuse and neglect went to a paper describing a support program to reduce "burnout" among child protective services caseworkers (Copans and others, 1979). As the authors and the review committee recognized, no solution to the problem of child maltreatment can succeed unless it expands the resources available to professional helpers. Our goal in preparing this book has been to serve these professionals by helping them see and use a range of informal helping networks. If we are at all successful in doing this, we will consider our time well spent.

References

Abramowicz, M., and Kass, E. "Pathogenesis and Prognosis of Prematurity." *New England Journal of Medicine,* 1966, *275,* 16-19.

Ahlbert, L., and others. *Revolution på Tjänstetid [Revolution on the Job].* Stockholm, 1975.

Aldous, J., and Hill, R. "Breaking the Poverty Cycle: Strategic Points for Intervention." *Social Work,* 1969, *14,* 3-12.

Axelsson, B., and others. "Man Bara Anpassar Sig Helt Enkelt . . . En Rapport om Människor i Skärholmen" ["One Just Simply Adjusts . . . A Report on People in Skärholmen"]. Mimeographed paper, Department of Education, University of Stockholm, 1971.

Bakan, D. *Slaughter of the Innocents: A Study of the Battered Child Phenomenon.* San Francisco: Jossey-Bass, 1971.

Banagale, R., and McIntire, M. "Child Abuse and Neglect: A Study of Cases Reported to Douglas County Child Protective Service from 1967 to 1973." *Nebraska Medical Journal,* 1975 (Sept.-Nov. issues).

Barnes, J. A. *Social Networks.* Addison-Wesley Modular Publications, Module No. 26. Reading, Mass.: Addison-Wesley, 1975.

Beck, D. F., Tileston, C., and Kesten, S. *Educational Programs of Family Agencies: Who is Reached?* New York: Family Service Association of America, 1977.

Behavior Associates. *Parents Anonymous Self-Help for Child-Abusing Parents Project: Evaluation Report.* Tucson, Ariz.: Behavior Associates, 1977.

Bem, D. J., and Allen, A. "On Predicting Some of the People Some of the Time: The Search for Cross-Situational Consistencies in Behavior." *Psychological Review,* 1974, *81,* 506-520.

Benjamin, J., and others. "Breaking the Child Mistreatment Cycle: A Study of Child Abuse and Neglect Programs in Douglas County, Nebr." Unpublished paper, University of Nebraska at Omaha, 1976.

Berkeley Planning Associates. *Evaluation of Child Abuse and Neglect Projects, 1974-1977.* Berkeley, Calif.: Berkeley Planning Associates, 1978.

Bibring, G. "Some Considerations of Psychological Processes in Pregnancy." *Psychoanalytic Study of the Child,* 1959, *14,* 113-121.

Birch, H., and Gussow, H. *Disadvantaged Children: Health, Nutrition, and School Failure.* New York: Harcourt Brace Jovanovich, 1970.

Bogue, D., and Bogue, E. *Essays in Human Ecology.* Chicago: University of Chicago Press, 1976.

Bott, E. *Family and Social Network.* London: Tavistock, 1971.

Brazelton, T. B. "Neonatal Behavioral Assessment Scale." In *Clinics in Developmental Medicine.* No. 50. Philadelphia: Lippincott, 1973.

Brim, O. G., Jr. "Macro-Structural Influences on Child Development and the Need for Childhood Social Indicators." *American Journal of Orthopsychiatry,* 1975, *45,* 516-524.

Bronfenbrenner, U. "Early Deprivation: A Cross-Species Analysis." In S. Levine and G. Newton (Eds.), *Early Experience and Behavior.* Springfield, Ill.: Thomas, 1968.

Bronfenbrenner, U. *Is Early Intervention Effective?* Publication No. (OHD) 74-25. Washington, D.C.: U.S. Department of Health, Education and Welfare, 1974.

Bronfenbrenner, U. "Who Cares for America's Children?" Unpublished manuscript, Cornell University, 1976.

Bronfenbrenner, U. "Toward an Experimental Ecology of Human Development." *American Psychologist*, 1977, *32*, 513-531.

Bronfenbrenner, U. "Who Needs Parent Education?" *Teachers College Record*, 1978, *79*, 767-787.

Bronfenbrenner, U. *The Experimental Ecology of Human Development*. Cambridge, Mass.: Harvard University Press, 1979.

Bronfenbrenner, U., and Mahoney, M. "The Structure and Verification of Hypothesis." In U. Bronfenbrenner and M. Mahoney (Eds.), *Influences on Human Development*. Hinsdale, Ill.: Dryden Press, 1975.

Bryant, H. D., and others. "Physical Abuse of Children: An Agency Study." *Child Welfare*, 1963, *52*, 225-230.

Burke, R. J., and Weir, T. "Marital Helping Relationships: The Moderators Between Stress and Well-Being." *The Journal of Psychology*, 1977, *95*, 121-130.

Campbell, A. "Subjective Measures of Well-Being." *American Psychologist*, 1976, *31*, 117-124.

Caplan, G. *The Theory and Practice of Mental Health Consultation*. New York: Basic Books, 1970.

Caplan, G. *Support Systems and Community Mental Health*. New York: Behavioral Publications, 1974.

Caplan, G., and Killilea, M. *Support Systems and Mutual Help: Multidisciplinary Explorations*. New York: Grune & Stratton, 1976.

Caplow, T., and Forman, R. "Neighborhood Interaction in a Homogeneous Community." *American Sociological Review*, 1950, *15*, 360.

Carkhuff, R. R., and Berenson, B. G. *Beyond Counseling and Therapy*. New York: Holt, Rinehart and Winston, 1967.

Cassel, J. "Psychosocial Processes and 'Stress': Theoretical Formulations." *International Journal of Health Services*, 1974, *4*, 471-482.

Caudill, W., and Frost, L. "A Comparison of Maternal Care and Infant Behavior in Japanese-American, American, and Japanese Families." In U. Bronfenbrenner and M. Mahoney (Eds.), *Influences on Human Development*. Hinsdale, Ill.: Dryden Press, 1975.

Center for Applied Urban Research. *Housing and Community Development in the Nebraska-Iowa Riverfront Development Project Area, 1973.* Omaha, Nebr.: Center for Applied Urban Research, 1973.

Cochran, M., and Brassard, J. "Social Networks and Child Development." *Child Development,* 1979, *50,* 601–616.

Coelho, G., Hamburg, D. A., and Adams, J. E. *Coping and Adaptation.* New York: Basic Books, 1974.

Collins, A. H. "Natural Delivery Systems: Accessible Sources of Power for Mental Health." *American Journal of Orthopsychiatry,* 1973, *43,* 46-52.

Collins, A. H., and Pancoast, D. L. *Natural Helping Networks.* Washington, D.C.: National Association of Social Workers, 1976.

Collins, A. H., Pancoast, D. L., and Dunn, J. A. *Consultation Casebook.* Portland Ore.: Portland State University, 1977.

Collins, A. H., and Watson, E. L. *Family Day Care.* Boston: Beacon Press, 1976.

Copans, S., and others. "The Stresses of Treating Child Abuse." *Children Today,* 1979, *8* (1), 22-35.

Cowen, D., and others. "Impact of a Rural Preventive Care Outreach Program on Children's Health." *American Journal of Public Health,* 1978, *68,* 471-476.

Cowen, E. L., and others. "Hairdressers as Caregivers. I: A Descriptive Profile of Interpersonal Help-Giving Involvements." Unpublished manuscript, Department of Psychology, University of Rochester, 1978.

Croog, S., Lipson, A., and Levine, S. "Help Patterns in Severe Illnesses: The Role of Kin Network, Nonfamily Resources, and Institutions." *Journal of Marriage and the Family,* 1972, *34,* 32-41.

Danish, S. J., and Hauer, A. E. *Helping Skills: A Basic Training Program.* New York: Behavioral Publications, 1973.

Darley, J. M., and Latane, B. "Bystander Intervention in Emergencies: Diffusion of Responsibility." *Journal of Personality and Social Psychology,* 1968, *8,* 377-383.

Daun, A. *Förortsliv [The Life of the Suburbs].* Stockholm: Bokförlaget Prisma, 1974.

Devereux, E. "Neighborhood and Community Participation." *Journal of Social Issues,* 1960, *4,* 64-84.

Eitinger, L. *Concentration Camp Survivors in Norway and Israel.* The Hague: M. Nijhoff, 1964.

Elder, G. *Children of the Great Depression.* Chicago: University of Chicago Press, 1974.

Elder, G. "Family History and the Life Course." *Journal of Family History,* 1977, *2,* 279-304.

Elmer, E. *Children in Jeopardy.* Pittsburgh: University of Pittsburgh Press, 1967.

Elmer, E. "A Follow-Up Study of Traumatized Children." *Pediatrics,* 1977, *59,* 273-279.

Epstein, A. L. "The Network and Urban Social Organization." *Rhodes-Livingstone Journal,* 1961, *29,* 29-62.

Fellin, P., and Litwak, E. "Neighborhood Cohesion Under Conditions of Mobility." *American Sociological Review,* 1963, *28* (3), 364-376.

Fellin, P., and Litwak, E. "The Neighborhood in Urban American Society." *Social Work,* 1968, *13* (3), 72-80.

Folksams Sociala Råd. *Vår Trygghet [Our Security].* Stockholm: Tiden-Barnången, 1975.

"Föräldrarutbildning: Utdrag Ur Olika Lagarbeten Och Utredningar" ["Parent Education: Excerpts from Various Legal Works and Investigations"]. In *Gotesborgs Socialforvaltningen,* unpublished manuscript, 1976.

Freedman, J. L., and Fraser, S. C. "Compliance Without Pressure: The Foot-in-the-Door Technique." *Journal of Personality and Social Psychology,* 1966, *4,* 195-202.

French, J. R. P. "Person Role Fit." Unpublished manuscript. Institute for Social Research, University of Michigan, 1973.

Friedman, R. "Child Abuse: A Review of the Psychosocial Research." In Herner and Company (Eds.), *Four Perspectives on the Status of Child Abuse and Neglect Research.* Washington, D.C.: National Center on Child Abuse and Neglect, 1976.

Friedrich, W., and Boriskin, J. A. "The Role of the Child in Abuse: A Review of the Literature." *American Journal of Orthopsychiatry,* 1976, *45,* 580-590.

Garbarino, J. "The Meaning and Implications of School Success." *Educational Forum,* 1975, *40,* 157-168.

Garbarino, J. "A Preliminary Study of Some Ecological Correlates of Child Abuse: The Impact of Socioeconomic Stress on Mothers." *Child Development,* 1976, *47,* 178-185.

Garbarino, J. "The Human Ecology of Child Maltreatment: A Conceptual Model for Research." *Journal of Marriage and the Family,* 1977a, *39,* 721-736.

Garbarino, J. "The Price of Privacy in the Social Dynamics of Child Abuse." *Child Welfare,* 1977b, *56,* 565-575.

Garbarino, J., and Bronfenbrenner, U. *Research on Parent-Child Relations and Social Policy: How to Proceed.* Working Paper Series No. 1. Boys Town, Nebr.: Center for the Study of Youth Development, 1977.

Garbarino, J., and Crouter, A. "A Note on the Problem of Construct Validity in Assessing the Usefulness of Child Maltreatment Report Data." *American Journal of Public Health,* 1978a, *68,* 598-600.

Garbarino, J., and Crouter, A. "Defining the Community Context of Parent-Child Relationships: The Correlates of Child Maltreatment." *Child Development,* 1978b, *49,* 604-616.

Garbarino, J., Crouter, A., and Sherman, D. "Screening Neighborhoods for Intervention: A Research Model for Child Protective Services." *Journal of Social Service Research,* 1977, *1* (2), 135-145.

Garbarino, J., and Jacobson, N. "Youth Helping Youth as a Resource in Meeting the Problem of Adolescent Maltreatment." *Child Welfare,* 1978, *57,* 505-512.

Gartner, A., and Riessman, F. *Self-Help in the Human Services.* San Francisco: Jossey-Bass, 1977.

Gelles, R. J. "Child Abuse as Psychopathology: A Sociological Critique and Reformulation." *American Journal of Orthopsychiatry,* 1973, *43,* 611-621.

Gil, D. G. *Violence Against Children: Physical Child Abuse in the United States.* Cambridge, Mass.: Harvard University Press, 1970.

Goodman, G. *Companionship Therapy: Studies in Structured Intimacy.* San Francisco: Jossey-Bass, 1972.

Gordon, I. J. *A Home Learning Center Approach to Early Stimulation.* Gainesville, Fla.: Institute for the Development of Human Resources, 1971.

Gottlieb, B. H. "The Contribution of Natural Support Systems to Primary Prevention Among Four Social Subgroups of Adolescents." *Adolescence,* 1975, *10,* 207-220.

Gottlieb, B. H. "The Development and Application of a Classification Scheme of Informal Helping Behaviors." *Canadian Journal of Behavioral Science,* 1978, *10,* 105-115.

Gray, J., and others. "Prediction and Prevention of Child Abuse and Neglect." *Child Abuse and Neglect,* 1977, *1,* 45-58.

Greer, S. "Urbanism Reconsidered: A Comparative Study of Local Areas in Metropolis." *American Sociological Review,* 1956, *21,* 19-25.

Gurin, G., Veroff, J., and Feld, S. *Americans View Their Mental Health.* New York: Basic Books, 1960.

Hales, D. *How Early is Early Contact? Defining the Limits of the Sensitive Period.* New York: Foundation for Child Development, 1976.

Hamburg, D. A., and Adams, J. E. "A Perspective on Coping Behavior." *Archives of General Psychiatry,* 1967, *17,* 277-284.

Hawley, A. *Human Ecology: A Theory of Community Structure.* New York: Ronald Press, 1950.

Helfer, R. *Report on the Research Using the Michigan Screening Profile of Parenting (MSPP).* Washington, D.C.: National Center on Child Abuse and Neglect, 1978.

Helfer, R., and Kempe, C. H. *Child Abuse and Neglect: The Family and the Community.* Cambridge, Mass.: Ballinger, 1976.

Heller, P. "Familism Scale: Revalidation and Revision." *Journal of Marriage and the Family,* 1976, *38,* 423-429.

Holter, H. "Familj, Klass och Socialt Nätzerk." In H. Holter and others (Eds.), *Familjen i Klassamhället [The Family in the Class Society].* Stockholm: Bokförlaget Aldus, 1976.

Howard, J. *Families.* New York: Simon & Schuster, 1978.

Joint Commission on the Mental Health of Children. *The Mental Health of Children: Services, Research, and Manpower.* New York: Harper & Row, 1973.

Justice, B., and Duncan, D. F. "Life Crises as a Precursor to Child Abuse." *Public Health Reports,* 1976, *91,* 110-115.

Justice, B., and Justice, R. *The Abusing Family.* New York: Human Sciences Press, 1976.

Keller, S. *The Urban Neighborhood: A Sociological Perspective.* New York: Random House, 1968.

Kempe, C. H., and Helfer, R. E. *Helping the Battered Child and His Family.* Philadelphia: Lippincott, 1975.

Kenniston, K. *All Our Children: The American Family Under Pressure.* New York: Harcourt Brace Jovanovich, 1977.

Klaus, M., and Kennell, J. *Maternal-Infant Bonding.* Saint Louis: Mosby, 1976.

Kohn, M. L. *Class and Conformity: A Study in Values.* Chicago: University of Chicago Press, 1977.

Kromkowski, J. *Neighborhood Deterioration and Juvenile Crime.* Washington, D.C.: National Technical Information Service (No. PB-260 473), U.S. Department of Commerce, August 1976.

Lagerberg, D. *Föräldravåld mot Barn [Parental Violence Against Children].* Stockholm: LiberFörlag, 1977.

Lauer, B., Ten Broeck, E., and Grossman, M. "Battered Child Syndrome: Review of 130 Patients with Controls." *Pediatrics,* 1974, *54,* 67-70.

Laumann, E. *Bonds of Pluralism: The Form and Substance of Urban Social Networks.* New York: Wiley, 1973.

Lebsack, J. R. "Central Registries and Reporting Systems." Paper presented at National Conference on Child Abuse and Neglect, April 17, 1977, Houston.

Leichter, H., and Mitchell, W. *Kinship and Casework.* New York: Russell Sage Foundation, 1967.

Lenoski, E. F. "Translating Injury Data into Prevention and Health Care Science—Physical Child Abuse." Unpublished manuscript, University of Southern California School of Medicine, Los Angeles, 1974.

Lewis, J., and others. *No Single Thread.* New York: Brunner/Mazel, 1976.

Lieber, L., and Baker, J. "Parents Anonymous and Self-Help Treatment for Child-Abusing Parents: A Review and an Evaluation." *Child Abuse and Neglect,* 1977, *1,* 133-148.

Light, R. "Abused and Neglected Children in America: A Study of Alternative Policies." *Harvard Educational Review,* 1973, *43,* 556-598.

Liljeström, R. *Uppväxtvillkor [Conditions of Growing Up].* Stockholm: LiberFörlag, 1975.

Litwak, E. "Occupational Mobility and Extended Family Cohesion." *American Sociological Review,* 1960, *25,* 9-20.

Looft, W. R. "Conceptions of Human Nature, Educational Practice, and Individual Development." *Human Development,* 1973, *16,* 21-32.

Maccoby, E., Johnson, J., and Church, R. "Community Integration and the Social Control of Juvenile Delinquency." *Journal of Social Issues,* 1958, *14,* 38-51.

McGarry, J. "Effect of Random Intensive Antismoking Education in Pregnancy on Baby Weights." *Directory of Ongoing Research in Smoking and Health.* Washington, D.C.: National Clearinghouse for Smoking and Health, 1974.

Mann, P. "The Neighborhood." In R. Gutman and D. Popenoe (Eds.), *Neighborhood, City, and Metropolis.* New York: Random House, 1970.

Mills, C. W. *The Sociological Imagination.* New York: Oxford University Press, 1959.

Mischel, W., and Ebbesen, E. B. "Attention in Delay of Gratification." *Journal of Personality and Social Psychology,* 1970, *16,* 329-337.

Mitchell, J. C. "The Concept and Use of Social Networks." In J. C. Mitchell (Ed.), *Social Networks in Urban Situations.* Manchester, England: Manchester University Press, 1969.

Morris, P., and Hess, K. *Neighborhood Power: The New Localism.* Boston: Beacon Press, 1975.

National Academy of Sciences. *Toward a National Policy for Children and Families.* Washington, D.C.: U.S. Government Printing Office, 1976.

New York State Department of Social Services. *Annual Report of Child Protective Services in New York State.* Albany: New York State Department of Social Services, 1974.

New York State Department of Social Services. *Annual Report of Child Protective Services in New York State.* Albany: New York State Department of Social Services, 1975.

New York State Department of Social Services. *Annual Report of Child Protective Services in New York State.* Albany: New York State Department of Social Services, 1976.

Newberger, E. H., and others. "Pediatric Social Illness: Etiologic Classification." *Pediatrics,* 1977, *60,* 178-185.

Nuckolls, C. B., Cassel, J., and Kaplan, B. H. "Psychosocial Assets, Life Crisis, and the Prognosis of Pregnancy." *American Journal of Epidemiology,* 1972, *95,* 431-441.

Olds, D., and others. "The Prenatal/Early Infancy Project: A Research Proposal." Elmira, N.Y.: Comprehensive Interdisciplinary Developmental Services, 1978.

Packard, V. *The Nation of Strangers.* New York: Pocket Books, 1972.

Parke, R., and Collmer, C. "Child Abuse: An Interdisciplinary Analysis." In E. M. Heatherington (Ed.), *Review of Child Development Research.* Vol. 5. Chicago: University of Chicago Press, 1975.

Petersson, P. O. *Child Health Services in Sweden.* Brochure No. 124. New York: Swedish Information Service, 1976.

Polansky, N. "Analysis of Research on Child Neglect: The Social Work Viewpoint." In Herner and Company (Eds.), *Four Perspectives on the Status of Child Abuse and Neglect Research.* Washington, D.C.: National Center on Child Abuse and Neglect, 1976.

Polansky, N., and others. "The Isolation of the Neglectful Family." *American Journal of Orthopsychiatry,* 1979, *49,* 149-152.

Popenoe, D. "Urban Residential Differentiation: An Overview of Patterns, Trends, and Problems." In M. P. Effrat (Ed.), *The Community.* New York: Free Press, 1974.

Rein, M. *Social Policy: Issues of Choice and Change.* New York: Random House, 1970.

"Report of the Family Life Development Center." Unpublished report, Cornell University, 1976.

Riesman, D. *The Lonely Crowd.* New Haven, Conn.: Yale University Press, 1952.

Rock, M. "Gorilla Mothers Need Some Help from Their Friends." *Smithsonian,* 1978, *9* (4), 58-63.

Rosenblatt, A., and Mayer, J. E. "Help Seeking for Family Problems: A Survey of Utilization and Satisfaction." *American Journal of Psychiatry,* 1972, *128,* 126-130.

Ross, L. "The Intuitive Psychologist and His Shortcomings: Distortions in the Attribution Process." In L. Berkowitz (Ed.), *Advances in Experimental Social Psychology.* Vol. 10. New York: Academic Press, 1977.

Rush, D., and others. "The Prenatal Project: The First 20 Months of Operation." In M. Winick (Ed.), *Nutrition and Fetal Development.* New York: Wiley, 1974.

Ryan, W. *Distress in the City: Essays in the Design and Administration of Urban Mental Health Services.* Cleveland: Case Western University Press, 1969.

St. Geme, J. W. (Ed.). *Child Care.* Van Nuys, Calif.: Sutherland Learning Associates, 1978.

Sameroff, A. J., and Chandler, M. J. "Reproductive Risk and the Continuum of Caretaking Causality." In F. D. Horowitz (Ed.), *Review of Child Development Research.* Vol. 14. Chicago: University of Chicago Press, 1975.

Schachter, S. *The Psychology of Affiliation.* Stanford, Calif.: Stanford University Press, 1959.

Shereshefsky, P., and Yarrow, L. *Psychological Aspects of a First Pregnancy and Early Postnatal Adaptation.* New York: Raven Press, 1973.

Shuval, J. T. "Class and Ethnic Correlates of Causal Neighboring." *American Sociological Review,* 1956, *21,* 453-457.

Skeels, H. "Adult Status of Children with Contrasting Early Life Experiences: A Follow-Up Study." *Monographs of the Society for Research in Child Development,* 1966, *31* (Serial No. 105).

Slater, P. *The Pursuit of Loneliness: American Culture at the Breaking Point.* Boston: Beacon Press, 1970.

Smith, C. "Locating Natural Neighbors in the Urban Community." Paper presented at 73rd annual meeting of Association of American Geographers, Salt Lake City, April 1977.

Smith, C. A., and Smith, C. J. "Locating Natural Neighbors in the Urban Community." *Area,* 1978, *10,* 102-110.

Smith, S. M., Hanson, R., and Noble, S. "Social Aspects of the

Battered Baby Syndrome." *British Journal of Psychiatry,* 1974, *125,* 568-582.

Spinetta, J. J., and Rigler, D. "The Child-Abusing Parent: A Psychological Review." *Psychological Bulletin,* 1972, *77,* 296-304.

Stack, C. *All Our Kin: Strategies for Survival in a Black Community.* New York: Harper & Row, 1974.

Steele, B. F., and Pollock, D. A. "A Psychiatric Study of Parents Who Abuse Infants and Small Children." In R. E. Helfer and C. H. Kempe (Eds.), *The Battered Child.* Chicago: University of Chicago Press, 1968.

Susskind, L. "Planning for New Towns: The Gap Between Theory and Practice." In M. P. Effrat (Ed.), *The Community.* New York: Free Press, 1974.

Sussman, M., and Burchinal, L. "Kin Family Networks: Unheralded Structure in Current Conceptualizations of Family Functioning." *Marriage and Family Living,* 1962, *24,* 231-240.

Terris, M., and Gold, E. "An Epidemiologic Study of Prematurity." *American Journal of Obstetrics and Gynecology,* 1969, *103* (3), 358-379.

Tietjen, A. M. "Personal Social Networks as Family Support Systems in Sweden." Paper presented at Conference on Research Perspectives in the Ecology of Human Development, Ithaca, N.Y., August 1977.

Tietjen, A. M. "Social Networks and Social Services as Family Support Systems in Sweden." Paper presented at 9th World Congress of Sociology, Uppsala, Sweden, August 1978.

U.S. Bureau of Labor Statistics. "Autumn 1975 Urban Family Budgets and Geographical Comparative Indexes" (supplement to *BLS Bulletin* 1570-1575). U.S. Bureau of Labor Statistics, 1975.

Vital Statistics of New York State. Albany: New York State Department of Health, 1975.

Wandersman, A. "Participation and the Ecology of Human Development." Paper presented at Conference on Research Perspectives in the Ecology of Human Development, Ithaca, N.Y., August 1977.

Warren, D., and Warren, R. *The Neighborhood Organizer's Handbook*. Notre Dame, Ind.: University of Notre Dame Press, 1977.

Watson, E. "Trailer Court." Unpublished paper prepared for the Tri-County Community Council, Portland, Ore., 1970.

Webb, W. *The Great Frontier*. Austin: University of Texas Press, 1952.

Weiner, G., and others. "Correlates of Low Birth Rate: Psychological Status at Eight to Ten Years of Age." *Pediatric Research*, 1968, *2*, 110-118.

Weissman, M., and Paykel, E. *The Depressed Woman*. Chicago: University of Chicago Press, 1974.

White, R. "Motivation Reconsidered: The Concept of Competence." *Psychological Review*, 1959, *66*, 297-333.

White, S., and others. *Federal Programs for Young Children*. Vol. 2: *Review of Evaluation Data for Federally Sponsored Projects for Children*. Report No. PB-242 957. Washington, D.C.: National Technical Information Service, U.S. Department of Commerce, 1972.

Willems, E. P. "Relations of Models to Methods in Behavioral Ecology." Paper presented at Biennial Conference, International Society for the Study of Behavioral Development, Guildford, Surrey, England, July 1975.

Willerman, L., Broman, S., and Fiedler, M. "Infant Development, Preschool IQ and Social Class." *Child Development*, 1970, *41*, 69-77.

Young, L. *Wednesday's Children: A Study of Child Neglect and Abuse*. New York: McGraw-Hill, 1964.

Young, M., and Wilmott, P. *Family and Kinship in East London*. London: Routledge & Kegan Paul, 1957.

Zill, N., and Brim, O. G. *Childhood Social Indicators*. New York: Foundation of Child Development, 1975.

Index

216